FOLK KNITTING
IN ESTONIA

Nancy Bush

INTERWEAVE PRESS

Editor, Judith Durant
Assistant editor, Ann Budd
Technical editor, Dorothy T. Ratigan

Photography, except as noted, Joe Coca
Cover design, Bren Frisch
Illustration, Gayle Ford, Susan Strawn Bailey
Production, Dean Howes

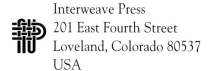
Interweave Press
201 East Fourth Street
Loveland, Colorado 80537
USA

Printed in the United States by Vision Graphics

Library of Congress Cataloging-in-Publication Data

Bush, Nancy, 1951–
    Folk knitting in Estonia: a garland of symbolism, tradition, and
technique/by Nancy Bush
        p. cm.
    Includes bibliographical references.
    ISBN 1-883010-43-8 (pbk.)
    1. Knitting—Estonia. 2. Knitting—Estonia—Patterns.
3. Estonia—Social life and customs. I. Title.
TT819.E76B87 1999   99-22927
746.43'2'094798—dc21   CIP

First printing:IWP:7.5M:1099:VG

Contents

Acknowledgments 4

Introduction 5

A Brief History of Estonia 7

Estonia's Folk Culture 11

Events in Life 18

Knitting Traditions 26

Estonian Patterns 28

Techniques 41

The Designs 56

Bibliography 119

Yarn Sources 120

Index 120

ACKNOWLEDGEMENTS

So many folks supported me in my effort to make this book a reality, it is hard to know where to begin. Each pattern in this book has been dedicated to a very special Estonian who has touched my life with friendship, kindness, and extraordinary sharing. Tänan väga!

I am honored to have been admitted into the special collections of four wonderful museums; the Eesti Rahva Museum in Tartu, with Ellen Värv as my guide; the Hiiumaa Museum in Kassari with help from Helgi Pôllo; the Royal Ontario Museum in Toronto, Canada with Anu Liivandi (my "first" Estonian) to aid me; and the Heimtali Museum near Viljandi where Anu Raud welcomed me. All of these women have shared their passion for their homeland, allowing me to study the collections of knitting in their care and offered invaluable assistance and friendship. A special 'thank you' to Kalju Konsin, who during his work at the Eesti Rahva Museum researched the knitting collection and wrote the most complete historic book possible on the subject. It was a thrill to meet him and share a discussion of travel and textiles.

As my command of the Estonian language wouldn't get me very far, I received monumental help with translating Estonian texts to English from Rita Tubalkain and Juta Beauchamp. Both have given many hours to this project, with their love for Estonia evident in every word. Translating from Swedish and German also came from my friends Kerstin Magnuson and Ursula Pimentel. Anu Kaljurand and Charlie (Kalev) Ehin, (both non-knitters) helped with translating technical Estonian knitting language. . . and, they survived!

Some of the texts I needed to learn about these knitting traditions came to me from Virve Mäesalu, Meida Jöeveer, Tone Takle and Merike Nichols. Merike's "courage" in inviting me to join her on my first visit to Estonia will always be treasured.

The language of knitting has been the major means of communication between Aino Pödra, Hilja Aavik and myself. I am sharing their lessons here in these pages.

On the other side of the sea, in America, I thank Marsha Thomas for her legal advice and human company on walks, Patrick de Freitas and Vonnie Wildfoerster for trusted proofreading and kind words, and Michelle Poulin-Alfeld for her help with technical questions, from solving mysteries to making them clear on paper.

Twenty six projects were alot to tackle. Luckily I had help from a "flock" of some of the best knitting friends anyone could hope for; Thank you Ann Carlile, Anne Carroll, Vicki Bourg, Lisa Sewell, Vonnie Wildfoerster, Melanie Elizondo, Linda Hansen, Betsy Campbell, John Yerkovich, and Ann Budd–you found my faults and made perfect mates.

To the folks at Interweave Press–thank you Linda Ligon for seeing the importance of this knitting tradition and giving me the encouragement to bring it to light; Judith Durant for your editorial insight and understanding of my dreams for this book; Ann Budd for your technical skills and expert eye to detail; Dorothy Ratigan for thoughtful questions and the checking and checking again to make sure each pattern is knittable; Stephen Beal for tidying up my words; Joe Coca for photographs that tell of quiet emotion and make each design shine with a Baltic light; Susan Strawn Bailey and Gayle Ford for perfect illustrations that give clarity to the techniques; and Dean Howes for making it fit beautifully between the covers of this book.

While doing all this work and meeting and knowing these extraordinary people, I also learned alot about life. My life has been enriched during the experience of making this book. Thank you to my Joe, for your advice, expert proofreading, support, and caring. And, especially for taking care of our garden, hearth, and housemate, Kloo, when I was away and for being there when I came home.

Introduction

Boring to live without beauty,
Sadder songless to be,
Woe to lack the lusting of larks,
So hard joyless to live!

I, myself, create my own beauty,
And harbor my dearest joy.
Beauty with me I carry,
Red hues in my apronstrings,
Joy tucked between burdens.

I would rather forget all sleep,
And leave behind my slumbers,
Than that I forget beauty,
And lose my dearest joy.

(Estonian Folk Song titled Beautymaker from the village Väike-Maarja, the translation was sent to me by Rita Tubalkain)

There is always great delight and satisfaction in making something useful and beautiful. The traditions these Estonian knitted treasures come from were of a harsh life, struggle, and worry as well as joy and celebration. The making of mittens or socks, or any other needed textile, is work–surely–but is also a delight, the colors and patterns adding pleasure to life and everyday events.

I discovered the knitting of Estonia while researching socks and stockings for *Folk Socks* (Interweave Press, 1994). I knew where Estonia was–nestled between Latvia, Russia and the Baltic Sea, and knew it was a unique country–never once thinking of it as "part of Russia." What I didn't know and what came as a surprise and quite a thrill, was that this small country was home to a fantastic knitting tradition.

I have always had a compelling interest in folk knitting and the history behind this craft; I sought out books about Estonian costume, history, art, literature,and crafts; any key I could find that would open up the magic door to this inspiring land.

The result of this quest is a passion for a place. This country has come to represent a sort of homeland for me. On my first journey to Estonia, I chose to travel by boat–to arrive slowly and be able to see the land appear on the horizon. I took a day–ferry from Helsinki, but spent the 50 mile crossing alone, outside at the railing, watching for land, knowing that something important was happening. When I finally stepped off the boat, it was like coming home, coming back to a land I'd never been to and a land where, as far as I know, my ancestors had never lived–but, this world is full of mysteries and perhaps, long ago . . . well, being of Northern European descent, anything could be possible.

In spite of heritage (or perhaps because of it) the folk art of Estonia seemed more than real to me, natural and friendly, joyful and symbolic all at once. I found myself rushing from one design to the next, charmed by the patterns and by the open, fresh use of decoration found on so many mittens, gloves, and socks. From museum to market stall, the very strong and lively knitting of the Estonians captured me and stole my heart.

This book is about sharing my delight. I found not only unique designs, techniques, wonderful colors, and a strong folk culture, but patterns that echoed other traditions that intrigue me; the X and O patterns from Fair Isle jumpers, Norwegian fishermen pullovers decorated with 8 pointed stars and Swedish Tvåändsstickning (twined knitting) with it's twisted threads. I have developed some theories, reflected upon by some of this craft's most respected researchers, about the diffusion of these designs, how travel and trade spread them throughout these northern lands. I also found a people who are passionate about their culture, who are kind and generous, and very proud to be Estonian.

This book offers a bit of Estonia to knitters, not only knitting lore, but history and tradition as well. I've tried to share some of what I feel about this place and people, and also to offer patterns to knit that are wearable in our time yet with a link to the past. I believe that it is important for knitters to know their roots, so to speak, to understand something about the landscape and the culture that created the environment for designs to evolve, to have a sense of where the inspiration originated. This is really my goal for this book. In some cases, I've reproduced a design, in others, I've been inventive. In doing this, I am inspired by Estonian knitters whose work seems to be growing and changing, open to new ideas or bringing elements of historic knitting together to create something fresh.

I have found that Estonian patterns are constantly evolving and the collection is growing even in our time of fast travel and cyber communications. There is a wealth of creativity and inspiration to be found there, from museum pieces to what one might see on a winter's day in the trolley, where the handknit mittens and berets on the folks going to town are, more often than not, breathtaking!

A Brief History of Estonia

ucked away in the northeastern corner of Europe are three small countries—Estonia, Latvia, and Lithuania, collectively known in modern times as the Baltic States. Estonia is the northernmost of these countries. At 17,000 square miles, Estonia is slightly larger than Denmark; 10 percent of the land is islands and about 90 percent is less than 100 meters above sea level.

A Finno-Ugric people related to the Hungarians, Finns, and Lapps, the Estonians differ from their Baltic neighbors, the Latvians and Lithuanians, in origin as well as language. Linguists theorize that ancestors of present-day Estonians came to the Baltic Region around 2500 to 2000 B.C., leaving the forested middle Volga region between the Kama and Oka Rivers west of the Ural Mountains, and following waterways to the Baltic coast. These tribal groups lived mainly by fishing and hunting. Their folk religion was based on animism or the attribution of a spirit or conscious life to material forms. They believed that spirits existed

in humans, nature, and beyond. Honoring these spirits brought security, good luck, and fertility in crops and farm life. Most ancient villages had a sacred grove of trees and sacrificial stones on which grain or animals were offered. (T. Raun, *Estonia and the Estonians*.)

During the Viking age, 800 to 1200 A.D., Estonians carried on commercial relations with their seafaring neighbors and occasionally joined in Viking raids. Their adventures took them deep into Russia and as far east as the Byzantine Empire. During this period, the Estonians progressed in the development

Photograph by Nancy Bush.

Farmhouse at Rocca al Mare Open Air Museum near Tallinn.

of animal husbandry and agriculture. The typical barn dwellings, consisting of a threshing room/granary and winter livestock shelter, a drying room (the only heated room) used for drying grain and housing the family in winter months, and smaller rooms for use in warmer times, were developed by the twelfth century. The country was divided into districts (*maakond*) and parishes (*kihelkond*) with no central government, but rather a group of leader/elders who united the people for defense.

Estonia's position, along the southeastern shore of the Baltic, made it desirable to neighboring powers. Hundreds of years of foreign rule began in 1219 when the Danes conquered the northern part of the land, founding Tallinn (*Taani linn* means Danish city in Estonian) on the site of the early settlement of Toompea. Needing help "converting" Estonians to Christianity, the Danes called on the German Order of the Brothers of the Sword (later the Order of Teutonic Knights), who already controlled much of the southern part of the region. The Knights not only did "missionary" work, but transformed the economy from one of agriculture and forest goods to one of efficient farming and commerce. Towns were founded and populated with craftsmen and merchants from Germany. German noblemen controlled most of the land, and Estonians were their serfs.

The Knights, along with the Danes and some powerful Catholic bishops, remained in control until an Estonian uprising known as the St. George's Night Revolt (1343–46) compelled Denmark to sell its share of Estonia to the Knights, making the Germans sole rulers. A medieval chronicler wrote that Estonia had become "hell for the peasants, paradise for the clergy, and a gold mine for the nobility and merchants." (L. Raun, *Subcontractor's Monograph on the Estonians*.)

The strength of the Knights weakened as the Hanseatic League began to flourish. Organized in 1358, the League was made up of a strong group of Northern German merchants who controlled trade throughout Scandinavia, the Baltic, and beyond. Cities on the trade routes between Russia and the West prospered.

Tallinn, today the capital of Estonia, was one of these Hansa towns and it became a hub of Baltic commerce, comprised of trading in grain, timber, furs, tar, honey, flax, and herring. The Reformation, which reached Estonia in 1523, also helped to weaken the power of the Catholic bishops and the Knights.

Estonia's advantageous geographic location and prosperity made the country very interesting to the Russians. Ivan the Terrible invaded in 1558, beginning almost twenty-five years of what was known as the Livonian War. Great devastation and misery were inflicted on the Estonian people, two-thirds of whom were lost. At this point (1582), Sweden, along with Denmark and Poland, stepped in. Sweden took over the north, Denmark gained power over the west and the islands, and Poland ruled the south.

By 1645, Sweden gained complete control of Estonia, inaugurating a period of better conditions and relative peace that Estonians called "the good old Swedish times." (L. Raun, *Subcontractor's Monograph on the Estonians.*) Land reforms during this time gave the peasants some of the land formerly in the hands of the nobles.

The German Baltic nobility, unhappy with the political situation and reforms that were threatening their power, joined with Russia, Poland, and Denmark to reconquer the Baltic lands. The resulting Great Northern War ended any hopes of more enlightened rule for the Estonians, and the Peace of Nystad in 1721 began a long period of Russian control, during which the German nobles were allowed to exercise power, own land, and lead commerce.

The nineteenth century brought some reforms. Estonian serfdom was abolished in the north in 1816 and in the south in 1819. Peasants were granted freedom of movement and choice of profession but remained unable to own land. They had to rent plots from lords of manors and compensate them with their labor. Several revolts occurred in the middle of the century, and by its end peasants had finally gained the right to purchase or lease plots of land.

The mid-nineteenth century is known in Estonia as the time of National Awakening, when a strong sense of nationalism produced pride in heritage, history, folklore, and culture. Estonians began to teach and learn in their own language, rather than German and Russian, and by 1900 there was almost total literacy. One strong influence on this period of awakening was Lydia Koidula. Born Lydia Jannsen in 1843, she became known as *Koidula*, which roughly translated means "singer of the dawn." She was a poet and writer whose words evoke her love and passion for her country. Instrumental in organizing the first Estonian Song Festival in Tartu in 1869, many of Koidula's poems were set to music. These songs have offered courage and unity to the Estonian people ever since.

World War I presented a difficult choice for the Estonians, who were inclined towards neither the Germans nor the Russians. The Russian Revolution gave them the opportunity to declare independence, and with help from the British Fleet and volunteer fighters from Finland and other Scandinavian countries, they did so in 1918. In 1920 Russia renounced its sovereignty over the country "voluntarily and forever." More than half of the land, which had been owned by two hundred German Balt families, along with Russian Crown Lands, was distributed to the Estonian people and 30,000 new farms were formed. Peasants were also given the right to engage in trade.

Estonian independence lasted for nearly twenty years, until the Molotov-Ribbentrop Pact divided the Baltic area between Nazi Germany and Soviet Russia. Annexation by the Soviets occurred in August 1940, and 60,000 Estonians were immediately conscripted, deported, or executed. When World War II ended, the

Soviets remained in power, and 70,000 Estonians fled to the West. Before the war, the population of Estonia was 1.13 million. By war's end it was 850,000.

The Soviets further forced their influence by creating collective farms, resulting in more deportations, a situation especially difficult for the Estonians who cherish a strong attachment to their fathers' homes and a great love for the soil. An organization called the "Forest Brothers" offered some armed resistance, but it was crushed in the early 1950s. Russians and others from Soviet-dominated lands began to take up residence in Estonia where they worked heavy industry and furthered Russianization. Estonians kept contact with the rest of the world through Finnish radio and television.

After World War II, strong feelings of concern for the environment and fear of becoming a minority in their native land spurred an Estonian nationalist revival, one that was aided by such groups as the Estonian Heritage Society, which quietly restored national monuments. Furthered by Soviet authorities in the 1980s, glasnost (openness) offered real hope for freedom, not only for the Estonians but for their neighbors as well. In 1988, The Singing Revolution occurred in Estonia. To make known their longing for freedom, large numbers of people gathered to sing national songs that had been banned. One in three Estonians (300,000) attended one gathering in Tallinn, a testament to the powerful emotional unity of the people. On August 23, 1989, the fiftieth anniversary of the Molotov-Ribbentorp Pact, two million people formed a human chain from Tallinn, Estonia, to Vilnius, Lithuania, to voice their desire for freedom. The culmination of this action took place on August 20, 1991, when Estonia declared independence; the Soviet Union recognized this independence on September 6, 1991. A constitution was approved in June 1992

and the Riigikogu (National Council), a 101-seat parliamentary body, is now elected every four years. The government is lead by a Prime Minister who is nominated by the President and approved by the Council.

Today the blue, black, and white flag of Estonia flies proudly over a free land. The colors were adopted from the Estonian Students Society, which was started during the National Awakening. "The blue stands for faith in the future of the Estonian people; the black represents the Estonian soil, the coat worn with many Estonian national costumes, and the hard past of the Estonian people; and the white represents hope for a better future." (L. Raun, *Subcontractor's Monograph on the Estonians*.)

Photograph by Nancy Bush.

The Estonian flag flies near the Alexander Nevsky church, Tallinn.

Estonia's Folk Culture

Estonia has a strong folk culture, one born of ancient spiritual and agrarian traditions that have grown and evolved through time. Country folk, whose society was rural, agricultural, and tightly controlled, created these traditions. The word for family and farm was the same in the ancient Estonian language and this farm society was the basis for much of the early cultural development. Village society evolved later under the Germans. Pagan beliefs lasted long among the peasants, even after the coming of Christianity, due in part to the fact that there were no Estonian priests and that the ritual was offered in a language other than Estonian (T. Raun, *Estonia and the Estonians*).

Lying at a crossroads of cultures, Estonia has been influenced by ideas from Western European, Scandinavian, as well as Eastern European and Slavic countries. Many of these customs, originating in a distant past, were begun with magic or religious intent. Through time, this intent has faded but the custom has remained.

Over the centuries, customs came to guide every sphere of Estonian life—work and play, relationships with neighbors or strangers, and the observance of holidays and events in family life. Much of Estonian experience was dictated by a folk calendar that reflected a continuing rhythm in life, the natural course of a year, from first snow to budding trees. Days for planting and harvesting were noted—"When the bird cherry blooms, then it is the time for sowing flax" (Tedre, *Estonian Customs and Traditions*)—as were

days of festival. March 12 was known as the "Winter Crest Day" (the day the snow had melted enough so that only the roads were covered and stood out like crests) and October 14 as the "Yellowing Day" (when the leaves started to turn yellow). With the coming of Christianity, days that were important in the old ritual culture stayed important, but took on new meaning according to Christian belief, and the two became interwoven. On St. Anthony's Day (January 17) "the winter was split in two and the bear turned on the other side in his cave;" on St. Michael's Day (September 29) "cabbage heads were said to grow so much that yarn tied around them would break;" and on St. Nicholas's Day (December 6) real winter was at hand (Ränk, *Old Estonia, People and Culture*).

An early method for organizing daily life was simply to count from one important day to another. For instance, "five weeks from Candlemas (February 2) to the melting of the snow, six weeks until the spawning of the frogs, seven weeks until the letting out of the pigs, eight weeks until the letting out of the cattle (animals are protected during cold months in this northern climate) (Ränk, *Old Estonia, People and Culture*). This system evolved into counting between holy days: six weeks from Christmas to Candlemas, ten weeks from Candlemas to Sowing Day, ten weeks from Sowing Day to St. John's Day, etc.

There were also two ways to reckon time based on nature: the solar calendar, which divided the year into four parts according to two solstices and two equinoxes, and the lunar calendar, which was based on the waxing and waning of the moon. Compared to the summer and winter solstices, the spring and autumn equinoxes were of little importance, considered only as transitions between the periods of warm growth and cold darkness. The winter solstice (around Christmas), marking the shortest day of the year and the beginning of longer days to come, and the summer solstice (around St. John's Day–June 24), marking the longest day and the most light, were primary influences. The summer half of the year included the entire agricultural cycle, from plowing to harvest, and the letting of flocks into the fields and protecting them again for the winter. The winter half was spent spinning, weaving, and knitting, among many other crafts and chores.

In the mid-seventeenth century, Estonian farmers in the northwest part of the country adopted a style of calendar from the Swedes called *Rimstav*, or calendar stick. Either six or seven wooden tablets joined together with string or a single long tablet, these sticks bore notches with Runic notations that indicated the day of the week and its significance. Crosses usually marked Sundays. October 14 (the day when leaves started turning yellow) was marked by a tree with drooping branches and April 14 (plowing day) is marked by a tree with upturned branches. The Runic calendar took into account the phases of the moon for timing agricultural and domestic work—waxing favored growth while waning marked decline. During the new moon it was good to shear sheep or cut hair, because both would grow again quickly. On the other hand, during the waning moon it was good to cut weeds or clean a room, because the weeds would not return or the room become dirty so soon. The waning moon was also a recommended time to plant potatoes—a waxing moon encouraged above-the-ground growth which would stunt potato development. Farmers transferred their vast knowledge of nature and oral

Photograph by Nancy Bush.

Calendar sticks with runic notations on display at the Estonian National Museum, Tartu.

customs to the wooden tablets and organized their year into a secure rhythm.

As for the hours of the day, by the seventeenth century Estonians were familiar with the sundial, and there was always the reliable cock, but it was really meals that partitioned the day for these farming people. In summer they had three meals; this schedule began on St. George's Day (April 23). Taking two meals a day began on Michaelmas (September 29th) and lasted the rest of the winter. "The time between two meals" (*söömavahe*) (Estonian National Museum) was an acceptable accounting of time. It was only in the nineteenth century that hours replaced the division of a day by light and dark times and meals.

Important days of the year were marked by certain activities, many related to the tending of animals and fields and maintaining the farm economy, but some also involved celebration and merrymaking. Once named for farm and nature, special days took on religious labels—usually saint's names—after the introduction of Christianity.

At first glance, it would seem that farmers often relied on luck to produce needed outcomes. But on closer observation, it's apparent that many customs had a firm basis in logic, also in the early belief that if one thing is taken from nature, another must be given back. Many customs are worth mentioning here, because they give an idea of the marvelous color of Estonian culture.

Photograph by C.O. Bulla, courtesy of Estonian National Museum.

Three generations of women from Jämaja carding, spinning, and knitting.

LADY DAY (March 25)

marked the end of winter and women's handwork season. If an egg placed on a fence post on Lady Day was broken by night frost, there would be forty more days and nights of frost—a cold spring. It was also the time when girls were "given the key" (a chance for some freedom and privacy) and allowed to sleep in the loft.

EASTER

came between Lady Day and St. George's Day and was also known as egg holiday or spring holiday. Eggs were dyed in birch leaves or onionskins and later in store-bought red dye.

ST. GEORGE'S DAY (April 23)

was named for the patron of cattle and ruler of wild beasts. Marking the start of the agricultural year at a time close to the spring solstice, this was the day that farm hands began their service; everything possible was done to insure healthy animals and successful crops.

It was believed that one should not go barefoot on St. George's Day, because the soil was still filled with poison and unable to breathe; if one did go barefoot, there would be bad luck with the animals. Nor should a woman take knitting needles into a strange yard, because she could attract snakes that would do harm during the summertime. One was careful not to make excessive noise while weaving or beating linen on St. George's Day to prevent insects and thunderstorms in the summer months.

ST. JOHN'S DAY (June 24),

marked the completion of many urgent farm activities that filled the weeks after St. George's Day. The atmosphere was festive, the diet more varied than during the winter months. On St. John's Eve, fires believed to keep witches from cattle

and fields clear of weeds were made in the center of the village or on a nearby hillside, while young and old gathered to make merry. Folk songs for this day offered a warning.

"The one who does not come to the bonfire on St. John's Day, his barley will be full of thistles, and his oats will be full of grasses."

(Ränk, *Old Estonia, People and Culture*.)

Young girls made wreaths for their hair from the blossoms of nine different flowers, weaving the wreaths at a crossroads and remaining silent after putting them on. That night they put the wreaths under their pillows and, with luck dreamt of their future husbands.

St. John's Night was a time for sorcery. It was believed that animals and trees could talk and that some people could understand them and learn what the future would bring. The magic didn't stop there—at midnight when the cock crowed, the fern would begin to bloom and whoever got the flower would have everything he or she wished for. But the flower was guarded by devils, making capture risky. This tradition survives to modern times, when young lovers go "looking for the fern blossom," hoping for personal happiness.

ST. JACOB'S DAY (July 25)

followed hay making and marked the time to cut grasses and herbs because after this date "iron nails got into the grass." (Tedre, *Estonian Customs and Traditions*.)

ST. OLAF'S DAY (July 29)

was a solemn occasion, marking the appearance of new bread. The first loaves or rolls were frequently saved and then served as an offering at the Yule festivities, often to the cattle. Even the first sheaf of grain was saved until Christmas, when it was used as an offering or to predict the future.

MICHAELMAS OR ST. MICHAEL'S DAY (September 29)

marked the end of summer and the beginning of winter. Field labor had to be finished by this day; farm hands were released from their labor, animals were slaughtered for food, and women started on their housework. Field workers said that "St. George binds you and St. Michael sets you free." (Estonian National Museum.) On St. Michael's Day, herd boys chased a white goat or ram three times around a stone to make the snow fall soon. Wedding festivities began on St. Michael's Day and lasted until the beginning of January.

ALL SOUL'S DAY,

which derived from the "ghosts' visiting time," was celebrated around November 1. Misty and foggy in Estonia, it was a time when silence was observed, spinning and housework was stopped, and ancestors who had left this world were remembered and worshiped. Food was placed in the sauna for the dead, to insure success in the new agricultural year.

*D*ear souls, come all along to have a meal, and when you leave, don't go across my field or along the road, but go across the bogs and marshes.

(Tedre, *Estonian Customs and Traditions*.)

ST. MARTIN'S DAY (November 10)

was a time for more festivities. The swingling of flax was finished and sheep shearing begun. (Estonians shear sheep twice a year, once in the autumn and once in spring before lambing). Beer was brewed, sausages made,

buns baked. There was much merrymaking to mark the harvest and the end of the farm work. Men would masquerade as Martin's buck (a male character who is described as "hairy and black"), visit the farms "begging" for food and wishing good luck, especially for crops and cattle for the new year.

*"H*ere I am bringing happy harvests, luck to you in cattle raising, let your pigs grow fat and pretty, let your sheep get sleek and shiny! Thousand suitors for your daughter, hundred sleighs behind the bathhouse, thousand sleighs behind the cottage"

(From the village of Rouge, recorded in 1938, Tedre, *Estonian Customs and Traditions*.)

The mummers were given food and a newly spun hank of yarn. Finally a feast was held that lasted for several days.

ST. CATHERINE'S DAY (November 25)

brought more mummers, usually female, disguised as Catherine's goose in clean white clothes. They sang and danced and asked for alms, blessing the master and mistress of the house. In eastern Estonia, young people went "bleating" on St. Catherine's Day. They would visit the shed where sheep were kept or come to the door of the house. The louder the noise they made, the better the sheep would grow.

ST. ANDREW'S DAY (November 30)

was the official beginning of winter.

St. Thomas' Day (December 21)

began the Yuletide holidays. There are many traditions associated with this time of year, some for pleasure, others to bring good luck to the farm. Centered on the winter equinox, these festive times originated long before Christianity came to Estonia. The word "Yuletide" (*jõulud* in Estonian) itself has its origins in pre-Christian Scandinavia.

Special beer and Yuletide cooking marked the festivities. Christmas trees are relatively recent, brought in with other German Christian customs. In the older tradition, families covered the floor with straw, then sat down to play games, drink beer, and tell stories and riddles.

Mummers made the rounds at Yuletide, disguised as geese, bucks, or goats. The goat or buck was dressed in a coat turned inside out, with a switch for a tail. He was sometimes joined by "shepherds," and the whole troupe would go from farm to farm offering good wishes, receiving in exchange beer, boiled beans, knitted socks or mittens, or woven garters hung on the mummer's horns (made with spoons or branches).

"May the girls get married, the hens lay eggs, the sheep beget twin lambs, the horses get male colts."

(Ränk, *Old Estonia, People and Culture*.)

New Year

became an official holiday in 1651 and, because it comes in the middle of the Yuletide celebrations, is sometimes known as the Second Christmas. The traditions for this day are similar to those at Christmas, but fortunes are also told from the shapes of hot lead or wax poured into water. A custom from the village of Jüri was that at the New Year, a girl would stand with her back to the door and throw her shoe toward it. If the shoe landed with the toe toward the door, she would marry during the next year; if the heel were toward the door, she would not marry. Visits were made on New Year's Day. If the first visitor was a man, luck would come to the house for the next year. A woman as first visitor was a bad omen, but if she were scolded, the bad luck would be chased away. It was also believed that a starlit New Year's Eve would mean plentiful births of domestic animals, and hoarfrost in the forest would bring a good harvest.

Twelfth Day or Epiphany (January 6)

marked the end of Yuletide in the eastern part of the land. Epiphany was the end of the holidays, the time when the Yule straw was taken out of the house and the spinning wheels brought in. Now work began in the woods with the felling of trees and moving of logs; woodwork and all kinds of handwork were done inside the house.

Candlemas (February 2)

marked the end of Yuletide in the western part of the land and on the islands.

St. Anthony's Day (January 17)

dedicated to two saints of the same name, was another day spent caring for the welfare of the farm. One St. Anthony is the patron of pigs, and his day is sometimes symbolized on the runic wooden calendar with a pig. Pig's head was cooked on this day, and was believed to promote luck with pigs (not for the one particular pig, however), cattle, and the whole farm. People did no work on St. Anthony's Day, believing that the pigs and sheep would not survive the summer if they did. Special bread was made and saved until the cattle were first let out in the spring. On that day, the bread was divided among the cattle to promote health for them and also luck in fishing.

Midwinter

arrived at the end of January or beginning of February, and it marked the time when all spinning should be done and the weaving begun. This was also time to account for all the provisions of humans and animals; half should remain. A symbolic midwinter gesture was taking manure into the fields to ensure fertility.

Shrove Tuesday

which we know as Mardi Gras, was the most popular day for celebrating midwinter. Since this day always has a new moon, it promoted growth. It was also the day that young oxen were first put in harness.

One of the most important Shrove Tuesday customs was furthering the growth of flax (for linen fiber). It was believed that icicles hanging from the eves predicted good growth for flax. In some places called "Sliding Day,"

Shrove Tuesday called for long sleigh rides to other villages to insure long-stalked flax in the next harvest—the longer the ride, the longer the stalk. Sliding down hills on sleds also carried out this custom.

"*Flax to those who go a-sleighing, tow to those who push the sledges, chaff to those who're browsing indoors!*"

(From the village of Vaivara, recorded in 1895, Tedre, *Estonian Customs and Traditions*.)

Another Shrove Tuesday custom concerned the "wild one." This was a straw person, dressed like a man or woman, sent beyond the village boundaries in a noisy carnival procession. The intent was to expel evil from the village, to protect the herd from wild beasts, and to increase luck with cattle and fishing.

After Shrove Tuesday, the year's cycle of celebrations, merrymaking, and endless backbreaking toil began once again.

Photograph by O. Kallas, courtesy of Estonian National Museum.

Knitting is as much a way of life as farming in Estonia. Note the woman in the center, and also the mittens hung over the man't belt to her left. This photograph was taken on Kihnu in 1894.

EVENTS IN LIFE

Major events in life mark the passage of time, and traces of ancient rites continue to this day. Knitting and handknitted garments played a part in christenings, courtship, and engagements and even saw people into the next life. Knitting was especially strong in the nineteenth century, and it is from that period that much of the information and tradition has been preserved. Each region has different customs, and some of them are presented here.

Birth and Childhood

While any child was welcome, boys were hoped for because they were added labor on the farm and brought more when they married. Certain handcraft tools, men's or women's, were placed above the expectant mother's bed to influence the baby's sex. Some days of birth offered more luck than others; a baby born in the evening was thought to be lucky, while a morning baby would have to work hard all through life. The moon, too, was considered. A boy born with the new moon would be wealthy, handsome, and clever, and a new-moon girl would marry young. The waning moon offered a baby poor prospects for marriage, wealth, or health.

These newcomers were protected by godparents whose obligations ranged from simply giving the child presents on special occasions to taking care of the child if it was orphaned. Upon accepting these responsibilities, godparents were presented with knitted mittens and stockings.

Boys and girls came of age at confirmation, paying for the necessary education by bringing the pastor coins, food, yarn, or firewood. Once confirmed, the young were allowed to play at mumming on St. Martin's Day and get involved in other frolic—and hard work as well. Because space in main dwellings was limited, girls would go into the loft to sleep. The boys would come visiting, beginning courtships that hopefully would lead to marriage.

Marriage Customs

When a young man decided to go courting, the first step was to sound out the girl and her family. This job was often given to a member of his family, usually an elderly woman, his mother or the wife of his future best man. She visited the prospective bride and her family, taking with her a bottle of spirits as a gift. If the bottle was returned full, the suitor had to keep looking for a wife. If it was returned empty with a pair of mittens or socks tied around it with a woven garter or belt, he was accepted.

The next step, if all went well, was to arrange the wedding. The groom visited the girl's family with his best man (*Isamees*), who had to be a married man. They took presents and special spirits sweetened with burnt sugar. The girl and her parents drank from the bottle as a final sign that all was well. The group dined and exchanged presents, perhaps a holdover from times when wives were bought. The bride might receive a silk scarf, knife, ring, or perhaps an apron; sometimes her mother and sisters also received gifts.

The best man and the suitor often went away with gifts of mittens; sometimes mittens, woven belts, or stockings were sent along to the suitor's parents. The belts were narrow blue or red bands or ribbons, usually handwoven on a small or rigid heddle loom, card woven, or finger braided. These belts were used as garters, tied at the knee of stockings with the ends hanging down as fringe. The patterns on these woven belts often inspired knitted patterns on stockings or mittens.

An Estonian bride had to fill her dowry chest with stockings, mittens, and belts by her wedding day. The bride gave many gifts to the bridegroom and his family and to the groom's men and bride's ladies, the musicians, and wedding officials. "A bride of average means needed around fifty pairs of mittens and a hundred belts as well as socks, stockings, and other small items of clothing." (Tedre, *Estonian Customs and Traditions*.) Mothers started collecting these items for their daughters before they were born. There was a saying that "a daughter one foot tall should have a present chest half a foot high." (Estonian National Museum.) Because these items were displayed during festivities, every effort was made to produce beautiful work as a matter of pride. A girl started making items for her dowry chest when she was young, and serious work commenced after the engagement was made and the first banns were read. At this point, friends and family helped by adding their work to the chest.

Another way to help fill dowry chests was called "chasing the wolf's tail." The bride went gift or alms

Photograph by Nancy Bush.

A bride's dowry chest was filled with stockings, mittens, and belts. This chest and wooden boxes are on display at the Estonian National Museum in Tartu.

hunting, a custom that dates to at least the seventeenth century. In some places she went alone, in others she was escorted. She took along a bottle of "engagement wine" (*kosjaviina*) and offered it to friends and neighbors who then gave her wool—more rarely flax, hemp, or tow—and in later times ready-made stockings and mittens.

Weddings lasted several days, with the new moon preferred. Celebrations were often held in two parts, one at the bride's home and one at the groom's home. The church ceremony was not as closely connected to the wedding as one would imagine, sometimes coming a week or so before the actual festivities. The church group was small and often included only the best man and groom's man, the matron and a bridesmaid, and the couple to be married.

Like much of the rest of life in these times, superstitions followed the couple to church. It was a bad omen if the first person they met on the road was a woman, and the bride was not to take a single needle

Photograph courtesy of Estonian National Museum.

The bride was covered with a large woolen shawl called a sōba or a linen one called a palajas. This bride and groom are from the Setu region.

bread, and perhaps a coin, because all three had strong powers to repel evil. (Tedre, *Estonian Customs and Traditions.*)

At the beginning of the real wedding, the groom's people traveled to the bride's home, where the bride was hidden away. Only after a meal was offered and perhaps a few bites taken did the guests demand to see her. Either the bride was brought from her hiding place or the women were led to her and given woven belts before escorting her to the groom. Or perhaps the bride and her friends were hidden under a sheet and it was up to the groom and his friends to find her. Sometimes a false bride, a bridesmaid, or a man dressed in women's clothing, would be offered. This was done with much comedy.

A complete meal followed the finding of the bride. In some districts, the couple ate wearing gloves, if they ate at all. In Setu the groom wore knitted mittens all day. And the brewers wore red mittens while making the wedding beer, to ensure that it looked and tasted its best!

or pin, for fear that the marriage would be a thorny one. The couple should not shake anyone's hand before the ceremony, for fear of handing over their luck. The bride carried with her a bit of salt, a piece of

In South Estonia the bride was covered with a large woolen shawl or *sōba*—the linen version was called a *palajas*—which was not removed until she was coiffed as a married woman. In the western part of the mainland and on the islands, this stole was smaller and known as "bride's sheet." (Ränk, *Old Estonia, People and Culture*.) In the time between the church ceremony and the home rituals, the bride wore a fur cap that indicated she was no longer a girl, but not yet a wife. At the end of the eighteenth century, A.W. Hupel, pastor of Põltsmaa, noted that graying unmarried women asked permission to wear the headgear of a wife in order to avoid having to work as a servant at the manor. Unmarried girls who were expecting or already had a child were also given this type of head covering to avoid shame. (Ränk, *Old Estonia, People and Culture*.)

The bride usually left her home in the evening or early morning. Songs sung along the way advised her that her youth was past and her new life would be one of worries, that she had to work hard and obey. The bride was often covered with the large shawl for this journey, to prevent her from finding her way home again and to protect her from the "evil eye." As the groom's people left the bride's home, the men, or sometimes everyone, were given gifts of woven belts. Ashes were taken from the bride's hearth to be scattered on the groom's, to stop the bride from homesickness. If she looked back at her home, her children would take after her. During the journey she dropped a garter at a crossroads to offer protection for her cattle.

The best man announced the bride's arrival at the groom's home, and the procession was given beer. None could be spilled or the marriage would be childless. The beer that remained was splashed on the horse that had pulled the bride's carriage or tossed in all four directions, the holdover of an ancient sacrifice. The horse was let into the yard through a hole in the fence rather than the gate, to keep him from finding his way out again. Mittens might have been tied to the shaft-bow

of the horse and the one that removed it received them. The groom's father, one of the groom's men, or the groom himself lifted the bride from the carriage and placed her on a fur or colorful woven blanket on the ground. This was to bring good luck and fertility to the marriage and the farm. The bride then placed a belt, mittens, or stockings on the blanket. As she went into the house—never left foot first—the groom's man made a cross in every corner to keep away evil, and at every threshold the bride left a pair of mittens. At the table, the bride and groom shared a piece of bread with butter and salt; sometimes she was given a child, usually a boy, to hold. This gesture ensured fertility and the child received a pair of mittens or stockings.

A sign that she was now a wife with a wife's duties, the coifing of the bride was central to most weddings. The mother-in-law placed the coif on the bride's head, perhaps reciting "Forget sleep, remember your husband." (Tedre, *Estonian Customs and Traditions*.) This was done three times, with the bride shaking off the coif until the third attempt. Then she was lifted up from the life of a maid to one of a woman. She was supposed to cry during this ceremony, to avoid crying later in life.

The chronicler Thomas Hjärne reported that at the end of the seventeenth century some women actually shaved their heads when they married. A church record of about the same time confirms this custom. "On the eve of the wedding day, the hair of the bride was completely cut off, as wives they did not grow their hair, but shaved their heads with a knife." Married women also kept short hair. (Ränk, *Old Estonia, People and Culture*.) This custom clearly defined the role of girl versus married woman and symbolized the subordination of the wife to her husband.

In some places, the new bride was dressed in an apron, another symbol of her new place in life. One way to raise

Photograph courtesy of Estonian National Museum.

The coifing of the bride was symbolic of a new life with wifely duties as depicted in this 1840 lithograph by T. Gehlaari.

money for the new couple was called "patching the apron." The guests were informed that the apron "needed patching" and money was thrown in it.

Now the bride's mother-in-law introduced her to her new home, showing her the rooms and outer buildings. Everywhere the bride went, including cattle barn and sheepfold, she placed gifts of mittens, belts, or stockings, which were later retrieved by her mother-in-law.

Among the songs that welcomed the bride to her new home, one from the region of Mulgimaa, asks her to provide handwork.

Often the new couple spent their first married night

in the cattle shed or sheep cot. The bed was made of hay cut by the groom; the bride brought the sheets. The groom's mother or the matron (the best man's wife) or perhaps the best man and bridesmaid, led the couple to bed. In some places it was bad luck for anyone else to even see the bed, as this could cause the couple to quarrel. In other places the bed was tried first by the groom's men jumping on it. Sometimes the groom's man competed with the bridesmaid or matron in taking off the couple's shoes and stockings. The winner could strike the loser as reward.

Listen my dear spouse
Hear my darling bride
The storehouse needs your gifts
The rack asks for clothes
The chest asks for aprons
The barn needs mittens.
Listen my good woman
Hear my dear bride
My walls beg for white shirts
My rooms for many colored shawls
The stable for knitted socks.

(From *Mulgi Kirikindad ja Kirisukad*)

In eastern Estonia, the custom was to lift the groom onto the bed, then the best man, or another man, threw the bride to him. This man was given a pair of mittens as a reward. In western Estonia, advice to the bridegroom included wearing mittens on the wedding night to ensure the birth of a son.

When morning came, the couple was wakened with song, music, or simply noise. They left stockings, mittens, or a belt on the bed for the person who made it, and left money in the wash water for the person who fetched it; whoever used the water next would be the next to marry.

Finally the time came to open the bride's chest and give out the gifts, in some places after the groom or his man had placed money on the chest for the bride. Since mittens had the power to protect, a large pair was sometimes left on top of the chest to keep away evil. Everyone in the groom's family received gifts. A full gift consisted of stockings, mittens, and woven garters. A poor bride might give a "half gift" of stockings or mittens. Big gifts were a scarf, mittens, stockings, and a shirt, and an even bigger gift often went to the mother of the groom.

The bride was repaid for these gifts with metaphors and humor. She was promised a "meadow mown four times a year," meaning a sheep, "a harrow that works backwards," meaning a hen, or a "wind ship and seven fathoms of silk strings," meaning a cradle and diapers (Tedre, *Estonian Customs and Traditions*.)

Funds for the newlyweds were given toward the end of the ceremonies, with the two clans often rivaling each other to give the most. A custom from Häädemeeste, known as "raising bone money," was for guests to leave coins on the table with the crumbs; they were then wiped into a sieve and given to the cook or the bride. Dancing with the bride was another way to raise money. Her first partner, often the groom or best man, received a pair of mittens; subsequent partners had to pay.

Dancing often signaled the end of the wedding party. Other signals were the uncoifing of the bride, or the bride bringing her spinning wheel to the middle of the floor and starting to spin.

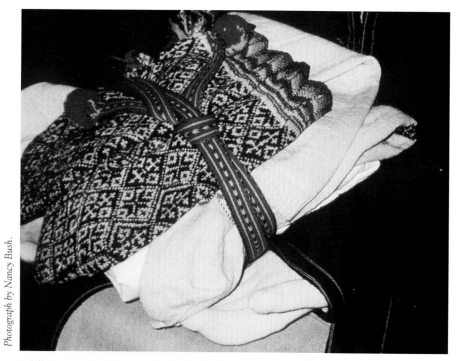

Photograph by Nancy Bush.

A full gift, typical of that given by the bride to her new mother-in-law, consisted of stockings, mittens, and woven belts. This gift bundle is on display at the Estonian National Museum in Tartu.

The End of Life

Estonian culture connected as many beliefs and omens with death as with life. The person who snored would die in summer when the carts clattered on the roads, but one who slept silently would die in winter when sledges moved over the snow. If an object moved with no apparent help, news of a death would arrive soon. The soul would be happier if death came in the morning; evil ones and witches passed away during stormy times. If death occurred at the waning of the moon, the departed took away the luck of the household. If the moon was waxing, the luck remained with the house.

In some areas people were buried wearing mittens; older women knitted their own burial stockings. The village people who saw to the dead—the casket maker and those who washed the body—were given mittens and perhaps the departed's clothing. In western Estonia, dreaming of white mittens meant that a neighbor would soon die.

Knitting as Sacrifice, Magic, and Medicine

Beyond the use of mittens, gloves, and socks as gifts or payment, certain beliefs dictated their use for sacrifice, magic, or medicine. In the area of Vastseliina, stockings were left on a sacrificial rock as an offering.

Mittens were used to choose a place to build a home. Three mittens were filled, one with grain, one with soil, and one with ashes. A child then chose a mitten. If it was the one with ashes, a new site was required; if built on the first site, the house would be in danger of burning.

To receive justice at a trial, the accused wore a pair of mittens knitted from yarn sheared from three different areas of nine different sheep. The Whipping Post or Devil's Post pattern knitted into the mittens helped the wearer avoid corporal punishment.

At sowing time, the first three or nine handfuls of grain were sown with a mittened left hand. This prevented evil influence. Travelers who lost their way turned their mittens or socks inside out to find the way again. Haircutters wore mittens or gloves so that the hair they cut would grow back faster.

As folk medicine, mittens and gloves were very useful. To help a sick farm animal, a left-hand mitten was filled with water that was sprinkled from back to front on the animal's back three or nine times. For persons with stomachache, a mitten filled with hot oats was pressed against the afflicted area nine times. Mittens were worn even in the summertime, looped over the belt, to protect the wearer from illness and the evil eye.

Photograph courtesy of Estonian National Museum

Knitting played a part in all stages of life in Estonia. This mid-nineteenth-century knitter is from Audru in Southwest Estonia.

Knitting Traditions

K nitting is a strong part of the folk culture of Estonia. Many parts of the traditional folk costumes were knitted, including gloves, mittens, jackets, caps, socks, and stockings.

Knitting probably began somewhere in the Middle East and migrated via traders, crusaders, and travelers into Europe through Spain and Italy. While the actual origin of the craft remains a mystery, the technique can be traced at least to the Middle Ages, when knitting spread throughout Europe.

Some of the oldest European knitted textiles have been found on Estonian soil. Among these many artifacts, most of which are actually needle-looped, is one item reported by archeologist Jüri Peets, the cuff of a

Photograph by Nancy Bush.

This nineteenth-century nålbinded mitten from Risti is in the collection of the Estonian National Museum in Tartu.

knitted wool mitten found in 1950 in a woman's grave in Jõuga in northeastern Estonia. The grave dates from the end of the thirteenth or beginning of the fourteenth century. The background was originally white with blue and red in a serrated pattern and one red stripe. The blue was likely dyed with woad and the red with madder. (Peets, *Mõista, mõista, mis see on.*)

The Crusades provide a likely explanation for knitting's appearance in this northern land so early. Upon their return from Palestine, the knights were looking for land in the Baltic region to settle, and they brought craftsmen and servants with them who, in turn, carried with them the knowledge of knitting.

There are reports of knitting from twelfth-century France; knitting has been found in Poland that dates to the late fourteenth/early fifteenth century. We know of knitted mittens from fifteenth-century Latvia and

Photograph by Nancy Bush.

Detail of nålbinded mitten.

sixteenth-century Sweden. The oldest known knitting in Estonia prior to Peets's find was discovered in a grave in 1936, along with coins dated 1667. These fragments of knitted mittens are decorated with some pattern knitting, indicating that skilled two-color knitting was practiced at that time.

Prior to the introduction of knitting, hands and feet were protected with strips of hide, cloth, or fabric created with the primitive technique known as knotless netting, needle looping, or *nålbinding* (Swedish). Foot wrappings were known in some areas up to modern times, and the needle-looping technique is still done today in parts of Northern Europe, particularly the forest areas. Nålbinded mittens (*nõelakindad*) were commonly made in Estonia as late as the nineteenth century, and some craftspeople continue to practice the skill today.

Nålbinding possibly dates to the Bronze Age in Northern Europe. One of the oldest known artifacts worked in nålbinding is a mitten dating from 200–300 A.D., found in Äsle, Sweden. Its high level of skill indicates that the technique was well developed in this area by this time. The Vikings, as evidenced by a stocking found at the Viking settlement at Jorvik (York) in England, practiced needle looping. Viking people living on Gotland traded mittens to Russia and the Baltic areas. Mittens were offered as gifts to officials in Novgorod. It is not clear how these mittens were made, but it is likely that they were nålbinded. The

Photograph courtesy of Estonian National Museum.

Typical dress for Estonian women included a "pocket" for carrying knitting, such as the one hanging from this woman's arm. She is from North Estonia.

technique was practiced in Southern Europe into the Middle Ages until knitting replaced it.

Nålbinding has often been mistaken for knitting, because both techniques have been used historically for mittens and socks. One reason needle looping all but disappeared when knitting became popular is knitting's "endless" length of yarn that saves the worker from stopping and splicing so often. Another difference is the fabric structure. Knitting can be ripped out easily, whereas nålbinding will not ravel and is difficult to take out. As worked by the Northern Europeans, knitted and nålbinded fabrics look quite different; nålbinding has a more crochet-like appearance.

Knitting became an important part of Estonian textile craft by the eighteenth century. A.W. Hupel's book, written during this period, lists knitting among the necessary skills for any housewife and notes that young girls should be able to knit by age ten. A typical Estonian woman's costume had a pocket for carrying knitting. Often these "pockets" weren't sewn into the skirt but were separate bags attached to the outside of the costume or worn hanging from a strap. On the mainland, most knitting was done during the cold season, after the fieldwork was finished. On the islands, knitting was done all year long, while walking, waiting for returning fishermen, or even cooking!

Estonian Patterns

One characteristic that I find most charming in many aspects of folk art is the *horror vacui*, or fear of empty space. The pattern motifs found in Estonian knitting generally appear rather simple when examined individually. But together, either as a repeat, grouped in a stack, or extended, they can be very ornate. Many of these patterns evolved from other textiles, woven belts being the most obvious source, woven blankets and rugs being others.

At first glance, it seems that there are hundreds of different designs in Estonian patterned knitting. A closer look discloses certain relationships in the patterns and a developmental link between them. The original motifs that are the ornamental basis for many Estonian patterns are often simple and usually repeated over the entire knitted ground. They may begin unconnected. When a square or net is placed around the motif, the original independence is reduced and the result is a new pattern. Sometimes the net is an entire pattern on its own. These net patterns are most striking when the background is dark and the pattern is worked with light yarn, but the reverse is also found. The smaller "strands" in a net pattern seem the most net-like and can be single or double. A tight net or grid results when a net pattern has diagonal lines running from corner to corner. There are often very prominent intersections where the lines cross and add another element to the design as a whole.

Some of the most common simple motifs are the dice, sieve, fly, whorl, and wheel patterns. The cross and the star, which often has eight points, are also important elements of Estonian patterns. These motifs grow or shrink or combine with other elements, such as the net, to make new motifs. In some cases the original motif continues to be recognizable, in others it evolves into a totally new form.

A more complex motif that appears throughout Estonian knitting is the forked or straddled legs pattern. As it evolves into larger or more ornate variations, it is known as the hundred legs pattern. This pattern has Slavic, Russian, or perhaps even Komi (a Finno-Ugric group living near the Ural Mountains) influence.

Many patterns have been given names. Some are common throughout the countryside, others have different names depending on the village or person doing the naming. Some names are of recognizable images in the patterns, others require a lively imagination to interpret clearly. With books such as Konsin's *Slimkoeesemed*, Estonian knitters today have an invaluable record of patterns, and names to associate with them.

Here is a small collection of patterns found in Estonian knitting. First are the simple motifs, followed by some more complex patterns. The patterns have the Estonian name, an English translation, and the village or district to which they have been attributed. Many patterns can be found in many different districts; ideas travel, gifts are shared, and brides cross geographical boundaries, taking their patterns along.

Simple Motifs

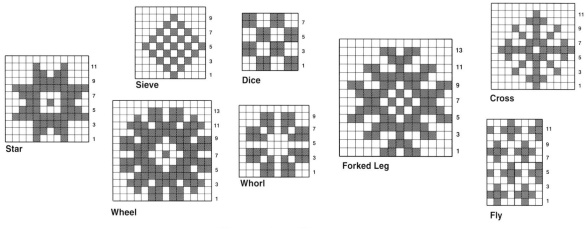

Star

Sieve

Dice

Cross

Wheel

Whorl

Forked Leg

Fly

Estonian Patterns

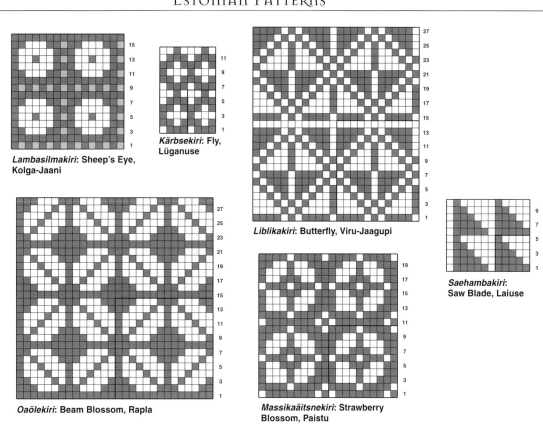

Lambasilmakiri: Sheep's Eye, Kolga-Jaani

Kärbsekiri: Fly, Lüganuse

Liblikakiri: Butterfly, Viru-Jaagupi

Oaõlekiri: Beam Blossom, Rapla

Massikaäitsnekiri: Strawberry Blossom, Paistu

Saehambakiri: Saw Blade, Laiuse

ESTONIAN PATTERNS

Kassikäpakiri: Cat's Paw, Helme

Lauajalakiri: Table Leg, Pühalepa

Põrsakiri: Piglet, Paistu

Ämblikukiri: Spider, Helme

Kitsisilmakiri: Goat's Eye, Helme

Kaardikiri: Card Pattern, Helme

Ubalehekiri: Bean Leaf, Paistu

Põrnikiakiri: Bug, Väike-Maarja

Estonian Patterns

Kassikapäkiri: Cat's Paw, Halliste

Põrgutulbakiri, Pessutulbakiri: Hell's Post or Whipping Post, Halliste

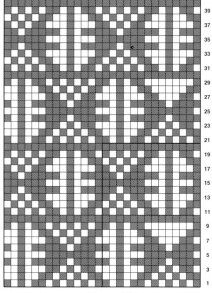

Vesikilgikiri: Water Cricket, Märjamaa

Põdrasarvekiri: Elk Horn, Helme

Estonian Patterns

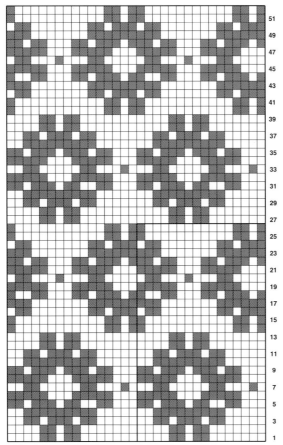

Rattakiri: Wheel, Helme

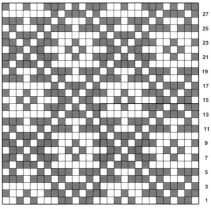

Vahtrelehekiri: Maple Leaf, Helme

Mittens and Gloves

Some of the most important Estonian knitted items were hand coverings, first mittens (*labakinnas*), then, by the eighteenth century, gloves (*sõrmkinnas*). The great importance of these items may be based on Estonia's northern climate, and may also reflect their use in folk traditions. One thing is known through written sources, archeological finds, and folklore: Customs related to mittens were originally characteristic only of the Baltic-Finno-Ugric people. (Peets, *Mõista, mõista, mis see on.*)

In addition to mittens and gloves, formerly nålbinded socks and stockings were improved by the technique of knitting. Shawls, scarves, hats, and later sweaters were also knitted, but not in such great quantities as mittens, gloves, and stockings. Of the nearly 4,000 handknitted items in the Estonian Ethnographic

Photograph by Nancy Bush.

These plant-dyed mittens from Muhu include traditional geometric elements—dots, squares, stars, crosses, and triangles. These are part of the collection at the Royal Ontario Museum in Toronto.

Museum in Tartu, the majority are mittens, gloves, socks, and stockings dating to the nineteenth century. Many accession notes record that the last owner received the item as a gift during a wedding. The museum's collection is a wealth of pattern, technique, and symbolism, as well as a wonderful record of Estonian folk costume.

Mittens are a very necessary item for the Estonian climate. A person needed many pairs, some worn over others on cold days, and one could count on wearing out several pairs during a long winter. Work mittens were made of rough, thick yarn, often fulled to strengthen the knitting and extend the life of the mitten. Finer mittens were made from softer fleece and thinner yarn. Mittens, gloves, and socks were and still are always worked using five double-pointed needles—four to carry the stitches and one to work them.

Up until the middle of the nineteenth century, when aniline dyes were introduced into Estonia, dyes were created from plants, bark, or moss. Red came from field madder or goose-straw roots. Birch leaves, yellow daisy, or chamomile were used for yellow and maple leaves and heather made green. Brown was extracted from pinecones, alder bark, buckthorn, or cowberry stalks. Blue was the hardest color to achieve; the indigo used to make blue came from India or Africa, was expensive, and was therefore used in small amounts. Indigo blue was known as cobalt blue or pot blue. The woad plant also yielded a blue dye and was much more available than indigo; it was known throughout Europe and Scandinavia and was used for blue prior to and even after indigo became available. Cobalt green or pot green was obtained by first dying yarn green, then over-dying it with indigo. Another imported color was insect red or cochineal.

One interesting way to color yarn was to wrap a hank with linen thread in several places, dye it, then remove the linen thread when it was dry. The result was known as "net yarn" (*flammegarn* in Scandinavia). When knitted, it had a mottled, tie-dyed appearance.

Most of today's Estonian mittens and gloves are made with two-color geometric designs. Mittens dating from the late nineteenth century and into the twentieth century may employ plant and animal designs based on older geometric forms. These designs are rather rare and are found mostly on items from Western Estonia, especially the island of Muhu, where bold aniline colors were used in knitting and in folk costume. In the rest of Estonia, even after the arrival of aniline dyes, colors remained subdued, the patterns often worked in sheep's black or pot blue on a natural white background or the reverse. Sometimes a bit of red, green, or yellow is added.

The geometric elements—dots, squares, stars, crosses, and triangles—found on most knitting are taken from traditional folk designs. Some, like the eight-pointed star, are connected to a magical past and carry strong meaning and power.

Designs on Estonian two-color mittens fall into several categories. Nature is represented by bird tracks,

Courtesy of Estonian National Museum. Photograph by Nancy Bush.

These colorful gloves are from the island of Muhu. Bold aniline colors were introduced in the nineteenth century.

stars, or snowflakes; the animal world by bear paws, butterflies, or spiders; plants by pine trees, strawberries, or maple leaves; location by village name and objects such as wheels or saw blades. Many more designs—windmill, sieve bottom, sheep's eye, piglet, beetle, cat's paw—also appear in the over 300 patterns collected in the Ethnographic Museum. Sometimes the patterns are readily seen, other times a good imagination is needed. The same design can have a different name from one geographic area to the next.

Designs were also adapted from other textiles, especially belts woven on small looms or with a rigid heddle, where a wealth of pattern and color was used. These belts (*vöö*) played a great part in weddings as gifts, and had many uses as straps, garters, and waistbands. It was believed that a tightly wound belt would make the wearer strong and offer protection from disease, so belts were even worn to bed. A belt protected the wearer from snakebites and boils. Woven belts had a fertile power and were often worn when seeding fields or planting.

Opportunities for knitters to see each other's designs came during social times, at church, or at market. If

Courtesy of Estonian National Museum. Photograph by Nancy Bush.

Colors were often subdued—pot blue or sheep's black on a natural ground or the reverse. These mittens from Löuna-Sakala use the elk horn pattern and have a short cuff with braids.

Courtesy of Heimtali Museum.
Photograph by Nancy Bush.

These mittens with the cat's paw pattern and peacock's tail cuff come from Paistu.

one knitter wanted to borrow another's mitten to copy, the left hand only was lent, never the right one, because it was believed that without the right-hand mitten the knitter would loose the ability to make the pattern. Patterns were also found in books and magazines, but not until the end of the nineteenth century.

These mittens, and later gloves, had a variety of hand patterns and cuff treatments. The cuffs of older mittens were sometimes practically nonexistent, only several rows of ribbing or simply a braided cast-on, with the body pattern beginning right after. In other cases, to be less stretchy and tighter to the wrist, the cuffs were made from a 1/1 or 2/2 ribbing, sometimes plain, sometimes twisted. Mittens from the island of Hiiumaa would have these short cuffs or, more usual, ribbed cuffs. Typical colors for mittens from Hiiumaa are white with blue, gray, or brown.

Longer narrower cuffs, even gauntlets, became popular toward the end of the nineteenth century and incorporated ribbings and lacy zigzag patterns. These cuffs were usually striped.

Very decorative cuffs with a bold "patch design" (*pôikilapiline koekiri*) were made using what we know as entrelac patterning, with small diamond shapes worked individually and colors changed on each course. A variation was serrated "fishtail" cuffs made with a slanting pattern and, sometimes, with color changes; these gave the same effect as entrelac but were worked in a very different manner. "Peacock's tail" (*vausaba*) is an openwork cuff with a scalloped edge.

Some cuffs had fringe, either at the edge or worked between rows. Mittens from Mustjala on the island of Saaremaa were very Estonian in character and color, with very long fringe and belt patterns across the hand. Fringed mittens, usually with a white background, were most often used by women. Men's mittens usually had a dark blue background. Motifs on both women's and men's mittens were very geometric, based on crosses and squares, worked in sheep's black with red, blue, or green lines. Women's gloves often had colorful patterns at the fingertips.

Fringed mittens or gloves were also found in other parishes on Saaremaa and on the mainland around Tõstamaa and Audru. These gloves had short fringes, half an inch long at most, used in the cuff to border other patterns.

Special decorative cuffs came from the island of Kihnu, off the west coast near Pärnu. These cuffs had a braided cast-on and contained lateral braids known as *vits*, an Estonian word also used for the hoop on a wooden beer mug. Vits were

Courtesy of Estonian National Museum.
Photography by Nancy Bush.

These wheel-patterned mittens come from Reigi on Hiiumaa. They are knitted in blue and natural wool and have a short ribbed cuff.

These roositud gloves come from Lüganuse. They have a peacock's tail cuff.

often used several times in a cuff, mixed with two-color patterning in simple shapes and diagonal lace stitches.

Another style of patterning for hand coverings was known as *vikkel*. This word has possible ties to the German *zwickel* or "clock" and may have referred to the clock designs at the ankle on the sides of stockings. Done in embroidery, this patterning was popular to hide seams in stockings cut and sewn from woven fabric. The decoration transferred to knitted stockings and gloves and continued to this century when it came to mean a solid-colored textured pattern where the stitches cross over each other one at a time. It could be worked over the entire body of the item or only in specific places. Vikkel-patterned gloves, whose popularity dates from the beginning of the nineteenth century, were more common than mittens and were mostly made with natural colored yarn—wool, cotton, or linen. Sometimes, as on the island of Muhu and in the parish of Paistu, the hand was made in this style and the cuff was decorated with a variety of colors. Gloves made with vikkel designs often had patterning only on the back of the hand and on one or two fingers and the thumb. These ornate gloves were worn mostly for festive occasions.

In *roositud* or "rose patterns," found mostly near Viljandi and the area near Pärnu, the color embellishment was added as the knitting was worked. The design threads were laid over the top of stockinette stitch to give the appearance of satin stitch embroidery. The pattern yarn was usually thicker—two strands of the knitting yarn, or one strand of a heavier yarn. (Knitting yarn was usually very fine, with 90 to 140 stitches for the hand.)

Roositud patterning is found only on gloves and stockings. The ground of the gloves from Tõstamaa and Audru was usually white, with inlay patterning on the back of the hand and several fingers or thumb. The little patterns on the fingers were called "paws." The gloves from near Viljandi often had a colorful background of red, orange, blue, or purple. The inlay designs covered the entire back of the glove, echoing belt designs with basic motifs of squares and stars. This type of patterning can be found on contemporary knitting in Estonia, but the

These gloves from Karja on Saaremaa have two rows of fringe and belt-like designs on the hand.

Patterned glove from Kihnu has vits or braids, two-color designs, and diagonal lace stitches on the cuff.

design is usually embroidered on after the knitting is finished.

The most common type of thumb shaping for Estonian mittens and gloves is the stocking or the simple thumb. Used for mittens and gloves, this shaping is worked from a slit in the palm created by putting aside some stitches (usually about one quarter the total of the hand) onto a length of yarn and casting on new stitches above them on the next round. Another method is to knit across the desired number of stitches for the thumb opening with a contrasting color and rework those stitches with the working yarn, keeping the established pattern. When the thumb is ready to be worked, remove the contrasting color, and pick up the live stitches to create the thumb.

If the color patterns in the hand are small, they are also used in the thumb as well. In gloves and mittens where the hand is a large format pattern, the thumb and fingers are worked in smaller patterns. Sometimes the back of the hand has one pattern and the palm another. Some gloves have a shaped thumb, with stitches added in the palm to accommodate the thumb. Often made by yarnover stitches, these increases create an openwork appearance in the thumb gusset.

Stockings and Socks

Before and even after knitting became a skill known to the Estonians, they protected their legs with long strips of woven cloth. Feet were protected with tow fiber (from flax) or softened hay placed inside outer foot coverings, or with foot rags—strips of cloth wrapped around the foot. These foot rags were made of linen in the summer and wool in the winter. The "shoe" was known as a *pastlad*, and consisted of an oblong piece of leather with slashes for laces that pulled the heel together and were wrapped around the leg. The front corners bent in to cover the toes. Foot rags came to just above the anklebone, and the leg wrappings extended higher to protect the leg. These cloths could be changed as needed, keeping the rest of the leg cleaner longer.

This custom of wrapping the leg continued even after knitted stockings and socks became popular. Hupel wrote in the 1700s that in some places, women wore short socks and wrapped their legs with ribbons. Sometimes they wrapped their legs and left their feet bare. Ribbons were

Colorful leggings such as these come from the island of Muhu.

Courtesy of Estonian National Museum. Photograph by Nancy Bush.

These typical stockings from Kihnu have pattern on the upper leg and vikkel clocks running down the leg and foot and are still worn today.

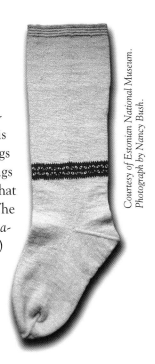

Courtesy of Estonian National Museum. Photograph by Nancy Bush.

These stockings from Halliste have a narrow band of patterning that is placed where now-obsolete leggings would have come, just above the ankle.

also wrapped around the outside of stockings for added protection and warmth.

These cloths or ribbons evolved into leggings, first made of woven fabric and later knitted. Leggings were worn like the ribbons. They were made of linen and worn with bare feet in summer and of wool and worn with socks in the winter. Women wore leggings in summer to protect their legs from dew soaked skirt hems resulting from working in the fields, and in winter to protect them from the rubbing of heavy woolen skirts.

Legging designs varied place to place. The most decorated were from Muhu and Kihnu, two of the islands to the west. Muhu leggings were often striped with a zigzag pattern at the top and were worn with short socks that were patterned with the typical Muhu Mand or pine tree pattern in many variations. Leggings from Kihnu were patterned with octagonal designs. With the arrival of aniline dyes in the 1800s, knitters on Muhu began to make colorful stockings, using orange, magenta, fushsia, and bright green along with other colors together in patterns. These were more figurative than geometric and included birds, scrolls, leaves, and vines.

Leggings were not totally replaced by stockings until modern times, and the women of Muhu Island wore stockings and leggings together into this century. The stockings that replaced leggings often carried a design that echoed the leggings. The shorter socks (called *kapukas* or half-stockings) and longer stockings from Kihnu have pattern starting just where the leggings would have begun. Kapukas are wide at the top and reach mid-calf. The patterning, worked in colors from goose grass, bedstraw, and pot blue, are inspired by belt designs. These half socks also have clocks on both sides. Mostly plain colored stockings from Karksi and Halliste on the mainland have a narrow band of patterning in dark blue, red, and green that is a "memory" of where the leggings would have come, just above the ankle.

Many Estonian stockings have wide belt designs on the legs and some are decorated with patterns from the ankle to the top of the stocking. Some of the patterns found in these stocking echo those found in mittens: paws, crosses, and the ever-present eight pointed star. These ornate stockings were mostly women's wear, while men wore single-colored stockings in

Women's stockings from Paistu with exaggerated calf. "The heavier the leg, the more lovely the bride."

black, white, gray, or blue. The men of the Setu region near the border with Russia wore colorful stockings with broad bands of patterning on the legs. These men usually wore their decorated stockings outside their pant legs. The color-patterned men's stockings from Viljandimaa, like the Setu men's stockings, often lacked a turned heel. It was said that "the foot will find it's own heel" (Konsin, *Slimkoeesemed*). Often the feet of stockings or socks were left unpatterned, as the use of precious dyed yarn and precious time to make a design that would be hidden did not fit into the scheme of a knitter's life.

Stockings also made a beauty statement, especially in the area of central Southern Estonia. A strong woman made a desirable wife and women wrapped their calves in cloth or tow, wore several layers of stockings, or did whatever possible to look strong, healthy, and able to work. They made stockings to wear over all this padding and, in some cases, the calf shaping of the stockings is very exaggerated. It was believed that "the heavier the legs, the more lovely the bride" (Manninen, *Eesti Rahvariiete Ajalugu*), and brides wrapped many ribbons around their legs to achieve this effect.

Roositud stockings, found mostly in Viljandimaa and Pärnumaa, are very unusual and decorative. Reaching at least to the knee, they have inlay patterns that run from part way down the leg, divide at the ankle as a clock, and end near the toe shaping. The designs are usually stars or diamonds and the colors are most often red and blue on a natural white ground. The knitters on the island of Ruhnu made a distinctive style of roositud stocking, with white designs on a dark blue background. This island was mostly populated with Estonian-Swedes until WW II, and this style of knitting may have had a Swedish, or a German influence. Another style inspired by Swedish and Finnish costume was the wearing of red stockings. These are found around the

Men from Setu wearing decorated stockings outside their pant legs.

coastal areas and such islands as Vormsi and Ruhnu where the Swedish population lived.

Vikkel-patterned stockings and stockings with allover textured patterns of single stitches that crossed each other were also known. These usually white stockings were worn for special occasions, such as when a suitor asked for his bride or for wedding celebrations. On women's stockings the vikkel designs would often be only part way up the leg, since the upper part was hidden under skirts. Eventually these patterns covered more and more of the stocking, especially those made of linen; woolen stockings were most often decorated with colored patterns. Men wore vikkel-patterned stockings with knee breeches and when they went out of fashion, so did the stockings.

Courtesy of Estonian National Museum. Photograph by Nancy Bush.

These roositud stockings from Kõpu have inlay patterns that run from part way down the leg, divide at the ankle, and end near the toe shaping.

Courtesy of Estonian National Museum. Photograph by Nancy Bush.

These vikkel-patterned stockings from Muhu are decorated with single stitches that cross over each other.

TECHNIQUES

Cast-ons

I learned to cast on my stitches over one needle, which is the most common method used today. However, most Estonian knitters cast on over two needles held parallel. This method produces looser and more elastic stitches, desirable qualities for knitted socks, mittens, and gloves. A tight cast-on will feel uncomfortable and can break. Some cast-on methods are illustrated here, and the choice of what method to use is up to you, the knitter; but I now cast on over two needles as a general rule, because the technique is compatible with the logic that prevails in folk knitting.

Continental method

This method, also called the long-tail method, creates a firm, elastic edge.

Make a slipknot leaving a long tail and place the slipknot on a needle. Place the thumb and index finger of your left hand between the two yarn ends. Secure the long ends by closing your other two or three fingers over them. Twist your wrist so that your palm faces upwards and spread your thumb and index finger apart to make a V of the yarn around them (figure 1).

*Insert the needle into the loop around your thumb, from bottom to top (figure 2). Use the needle tip to grab the yarn around your index finger, then bring the needle back down through the loop around your thumb (figure 3). Drop the loop off your thumb and, placing your thumb back in the V configuration,

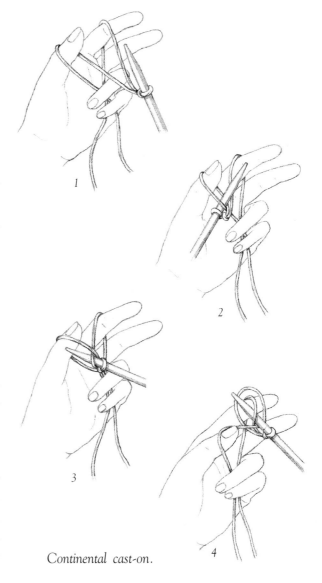

Continental cast-on.

tighten up the resulting stitch on the needle (figure 4). Repeat from * for the desired number of stitches.

Double-start cast-on

This two-part method, which combines the Continental cast-on (stitch A) with a similar motion (stitch B), makes a decorative edge and is commonly used in Estonia today. Worked one after the other, the stitches result in a double yarn along the front of every two cast-on stitches. You can work this method with one, two, or three strands of yarn around your thumb, depending on how prominent you want the cast-on row.

Set up as for the Continental cast-on (page 41). The slipknot will count as the first stitch (A). To make stitch B, remove your thumb from the loop and re-insert it so that the yarn wraps in the opposite direction (figure 1). Bring the needle under the yarn on the inside of your thumb (the yarn between your index finger and thumb), then go over the yarn around

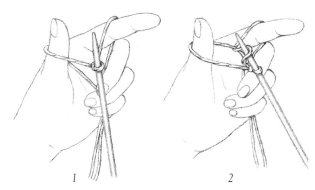

Double-start cast-on.

your index finger, and back through the thumb loop (figure 2). Drop the loop off your thumb and, placing your thumb back in the original V formation, tighten up the resulting stitch on the needle. You now have

two stitches on the needle: the slipknot and stitch B. (*Note:* Casting on with stitch B alone will give an appearance similar to the Continental cast-on, but the fronts of the stitches will angle to the left rather than to the right.) Cast on the next stitch following the Continental method. This will be stitch A. Continue to alternate stitch B and stitch A for the desired number of stitches. The stitches will be grouped in pairs on the needle (figure 3).

To cast on with a double or triple yarn, measure

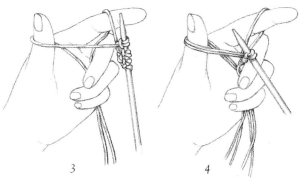

Double-start cast-on.

yarn for the number of stitches required, then fold the yarn and measure one or two more length(s). Make a slipknot about 5" (12.5 cm) up from the end of the short tail opposite the loop. When you begin the cast-on, place the doubled or tripled yarn around your thumb and the single strand around your index finger (figure 4). You will weave in the short end later.

Kihnu Troi cast-on

Kihnu is a small, very traditional island in the Baltic Sea. The closest town on the Estonian mainland is Pärnu. In addition to stockings, mittens, and gloves, the knitters of Kihnu also knit pullovers. These men's sweaters, traditionally decorated with braids and patterned knitting, are called Kihnu Troi. They are generally begun with the following two-color cast-on.

Work this cast-on with one light and one dark yarn. Tie each yarn into a slipknot. Place the knots onto the left needle with the dark "stitch" to the left. Keep the short ends forward and working yarn to the back. With the dark yarn, knit the light stitch (figure 1). You now have a dark stitch on the left needle and a dark stitch on the right needle. Bring both working ends to the front, between the two needles as you would to purl. Leave the dark yarn forward and to the right, take the light yarn to the back of the right needle, between the two needles as you would to knit, and *form a yarnover by wrapping the yarn clockwise (figure 2) around the right needle point. (This method is backwards from a conventional yarnover and will form a new stitch). Now knit into the dark stitch on the left needle with the light yarn (figure 3). Transfer the resulting stitch back onto the left needle. Bring the light yarn to the front, lay it over and to the right (aligning it with the right needle), and bring the dark yarn *under* it and to the back (figure 4). Tension the stitches by pulling slightly on the waiting (light) yarn. Repeat from *, alternating the two colors, until you have the desired number of stitches plus one. This last stitch and the one before it are both the opposite color of the first stitch cast on (figure 5). Distribute the stitches onto double-pointed needles, slip the first stitch back to the right needle, pass the last stitch over it as if to bind-off, then place the first stitch back on the left needle. The round will be joined and the colors will alternate all around. *Note:* This cast-on method produces twisted stitches that will need to be corrected when you place the stitches onto double-pointed needles or on the first round of knitting. You will also need to untwist your working yarns.

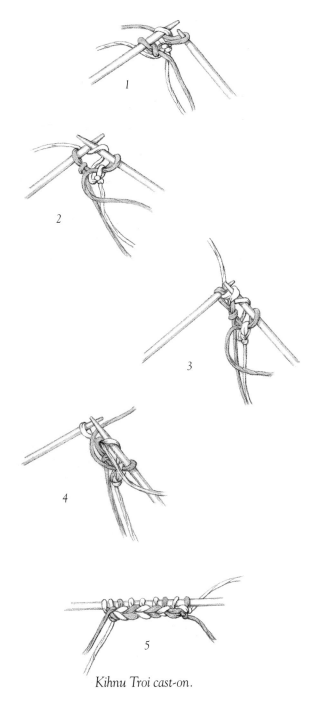

Kihnu Troi cast-on.

Liidia's braid cast-on

Liidia lives on Kihnu. I met her as she sat in front of her farm knitting a sleeve for a doll in the traditional pattern of a Kihnu Troi. I asked about her unusual two-color cast-on, and this is what she taught me.

Start with a slipknot made from two colors of yarn. This slipknot does not figure in the stitch count and will be dropped before the stitches are joined. Hold the two ends of yarn as for stitch B of the double-start cast-on (page 42), with the dark yarn over your index finger and the light yarn over your thumb (figure 1). Cast on one stitch (figure 2). Bring the dark yarn to the front and into position around your thumb, passing it *over* the light yarn, and put the light yarn to the back in position around your index finger (figure 3). Work stitch B of the double-start cast-on again (figure 4). Continue in this manner, switching the col-

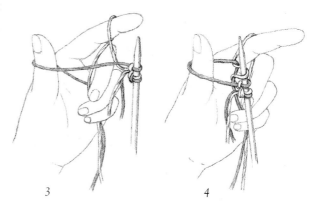

Liidia's braid cast-on.

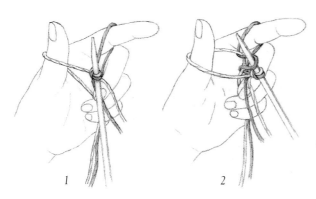

Liidia's braid cast-on.

ors with every new stitch. Cast on an even number of stitches plus one (this will be the same color as the first stitch cast on). Divide the stitches onto double-pointed needles and join by slipping the extra stitch onto the left needle and knitting it together with the first stitch cast on.

Fringe cast-on

A number of wonderful gloves in the Estonian National Museum have fringe at the base of the cuffs. The more decorative fringes are extraordinarily long and in several colors. Fringed gloves were probably used only

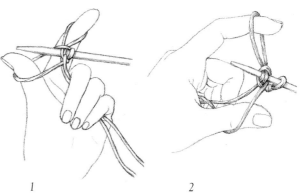

Fringe cast-on.

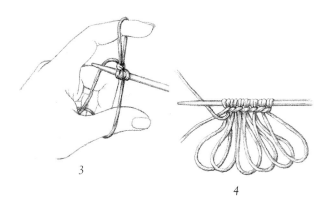

Fringe cast-on.

Backward loop cast-on

I often refer to this method as a wimpy cast-on. Also called a half-hitch loop, this is the most simple, yet not the most tidy, way to cast on stitches. Use it to add stitches at the base of thumb or fingers on gloves.

Place a slipknot on the right needle leaving a short tail. Wrap the working yarn clockwise around your left thumb and close your fingers around the yarn ends to secure them (figure 1). Holding the needle in your right hand, aim it upwards through the loop around your thumb, slip the loop from thumb onto the needle, and pull the yarn to tighten the loop on the needle (figure 2).

for festivals or weddings, since the fringe would be impractical while working. The longer fringed gloves come from the island of Saaremaa. Gloves from Töstamaa and Tori near Pärnu have shorter fringe and some have fringe worked into the cuff farther up from the edge. These fringes can be added after a piece is knitted or formed as part of the cast-on.

The fringe cast-on is worked much like the Continental cast-on, but the needle picks up both sides of the loop around your index finger to form the fringe (figures 1 and 2). With your index finger maintaining the fringe loop, tighten up the stitch by pulling on the thumb yarn (figures 3 and 4). Remove your index finger from the loop and set up again for the Continental cast-on. To work this cast-on with two colors, start with a slipknot made of both colors and set up as for a Continental cast-on with one color around your thumb and the other around your index finger. Switch colors at each pass, passing the front yarn *over* the top of the fringe yarn as they meet. This cast-on will result in two yarns over the needle for each stitch; treat theseas single stitches on the next round.

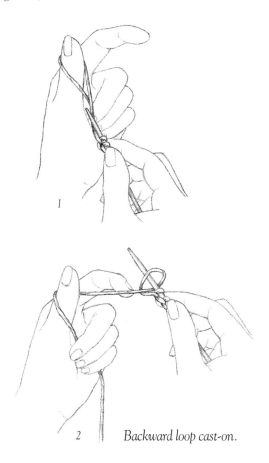

Backward loop cast-on.

Joins

After casting on the necessary number of stitches, divide them evenly onto double-pointed needles in preparation to work in the round. There are several ways to join the last cast-on stitch with the first, my favorite being the crossover method. You may find a join you like better.

Crossover join

Slip the first cast-on stitch (at the point of the left needle) onto the right needle (figure 1). With the left needle, lift the last cast-on stitch (which is now one stitch in from the end of the right needle) up over the top of the first cast-on stitch, and place it onto the left needle (figures 2 and 3). In essence, you have changed places with the first and the last stitch cast on, and the last stitch surrounds the first.

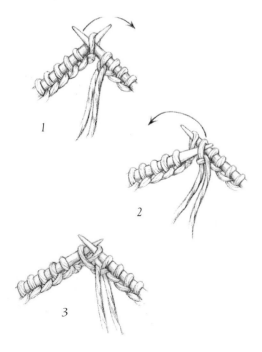

Crossover join.

Extra stitch join

Cast on one more stitch than required. Slip the extra stitch onto the left needle next to the first cast-on stitch (figure 1) and knit these two stitches together (figure 2). This will give you the required stitch count and a tidy join.

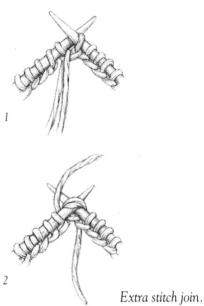

Extra stitch join.

Two-end join

Work the first two or three stitches of the round with the tail end (remaining from the cast on) and working end of yarn held together (figure 1). Drop the tail end and continue on with the working yarn. On the next round, be sure to work the double-strand stitches as if they were single.

Two-end join.

Decreases

The Estonians decrease by knitting two stitches together (k2tog), purling two stitches together (p2tog), or by slipping one stitch, knitting the next, and then passing the slipped stitch over (sl 1, k1, psso). As always, you may choose to use other left-leaning decreases, but I have used the most common Estonian techniques along with knitting two stitches together through the back loops (k2tog tbl) throughout the patterns.

Right-slanting decreases

K2tog: Knit two stitches together as if they were one.

P2tog: (Usually worked on the wrong side.) Purl two stitches together as if they were one.

Left-slanting decreases

Sl 1, k1, psso: (Slip 1, knit 1, pass slipped stitch over) Slip one stitch *as to knit* (figure 1), knit one stitch, insert the left needle into the front of the slipped stitch from left to right, and lift it up and over the knitted stitch and drop it off. *Note:* This decrease is similar to the ssk method (slip two stitches individually knitwise, insert the left needle into the front of these two slipped stitches from left to right, and knit them together through their back loops).

K2tog tbl: (Knit two together through the back loops) Insert the right needle into the back loops of two stitches, then knit them together.

Decrease to shape tops and thumbs of mittens and fingers of gloves

"Wick" decreases are direct translations of the Estonian names. One-wick and half-wick decreases are not commonly used elsewhere. The two-wick decrease is the same as the commonly known flat decrease. All these double-decrease methods are worked at the beginning and midpoint of a round, and are in line with the side edges of the mitten or finger.

One-wick decrease

This type of double-decrease works well with patterns that have an uninterrupted line of stitches along each side edge. This line becomes the center of the decrease, which is worked over three stitches—the center stitch and one stitch on either side. This decrease involves the last stitch of one needle and the first two stitches of the next needle.

To do a one-wick decrease, knit one stitch, pull this new loop up and place it on your left index finger (figure 1), slip the next (center) stitch as to knit

Sl 1, k1, psso.

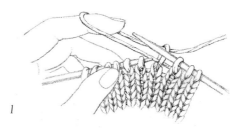

One-wick decrease.

(figure 2), knit the third stitch by catching the right half of the loop over your index finger and pulling it through (figure 3), tighten up working yarn, and pass the slipped stitch over this last stitch (figure 4).

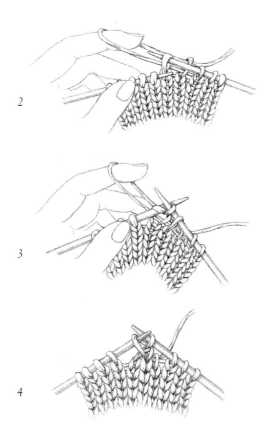

One-wick decrease.

Half-wick decrease

This decrease is good for patterns in which the back of the hand is identical to the palm. Work this double-decrease over three stitches—a center stitch and one stitch on either side. Worked at the beginning of the round, this decrease involves the last stitch of the previous round and the first two stitches of the next round.

To do a half-wick decrease, knit one stitch, pull this new loop up and place it on your left index finger as for the one-wick method and knit the next two stitches together with the loop from the first stitch (figure 1). The result is one angled stitch from three (figure 2).

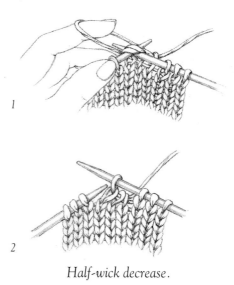

Half-wick decrease.

Two-wick decrease

This mirror-image flat decrease is used for tops of mittens, fingers, or thumbs where stitches are divided evenly onto four needles, with the side "seams" between needles #2 and #3, and needles #4 and #1. If you're working with an uneven number of stitches, you should have the same number of stitches on the first two needles as on the last two. In some patterns the decreases are worked with the same color on every round. In others, the colors are alternated.

To work this decrease, slip one stitch as if to knit, knit one stitch, pass the slipped stitch over at the beginning of needle #1 (figure 1), work to the last two stitches of needle #2, knit these two stitches together (figure 2), slip one, knit one, pass the slipped stitch over at the beginning of needle #3, work to last two stitches of needle #4, knit these two stitches together.

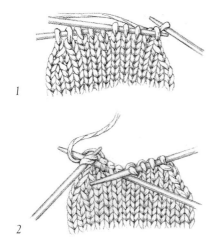

Two-wick decrease.

Braids

I was intrigued by Estonian knitting when I saw the decorative knitted braids used on cuffs and edgings. I immediately wanted to know how to make them, and thoroughly enjoyed solving the mystery. Each of the following braids is used in at least one of the patterns in this book, but not necessarily in all of the possible color configurations, which I offer here for inspiration. I have given my own names to the yarnover and vikkel braids, based on the way that they are formed. They may have other names in Estonian, but that remains part of the mystery. After completing a round of a braid pattern, be sure to count your stitches and adjust them onto the proper needles, since they can "wander" a bit during the working. All these braids work best over an even number of stitches.

Yarnover braid
(worked on an even number of stitches)
One-color: Increase one stitch by working a yarnover at the beginning of the needle. Then knit the next two stitches together through their back loops (figure 1), *place resulting stitch back onto left needle (figure 2), yarnover (figure 3), and knit two stitches together through their back loops. Repeat from *

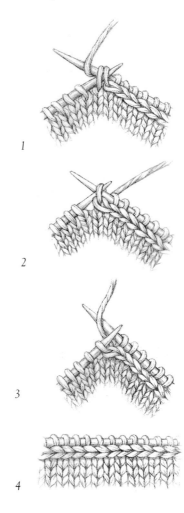

One-color yarnover braid.

(figure 4). *Note:* At the end of one needle, slip the last stitch onto the next needle. Also, as you work, remember to replace the stitch just made back to the left needle before working the next yarnover. On the following round, you may want to knit each stitch through its back loop to tighten up the fabric.

Two-color: Work as above, but begin with new color and alternate colors with each "yo, k2tog" set of stitches (figure 5). Tidy up the braid stitch before the next yarnover by tugging on the yarn you will use next.

5

Two-color yarnover braid.

Traveling stitch or vikkel braid

Vikkel is the Estonian word to describe patterns made with stitches that cross over each other and this lateral braid is worked in a similar manner. The braids are not worked with an extra cable needle, but by manipulation.

One-color: Increase one stitch by picking up the bar between the last stitch worked and the next stitch, and knit into it through the back loop (this is the same as the M1 increase). Place the stitch just made onto the left needle (figure 1). *Bring the right needle behind this stitch, knit the next stitch through the back loop (figure 2), then knit the first stitch through the front as usual, and slip both stitches off (figure 3). Place the stitch just made back onto the left needle, and repeat from *. *Note:* Remember to always drop both stitches after they are worked. At

the end of the round, pass the last stitch over the first stitch as to bind off to get back to required stitch count.

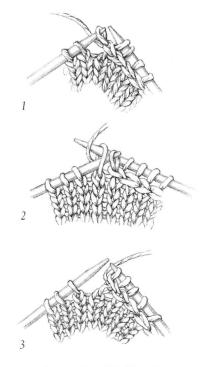

1

2

3

One-color vikkel braid.

Two-color: Work as above, but work the lifted stitch with a contrast color. Placing this stitch onto the left needle, *knit the second stitch through the back loop with the contrast color, then knit the first stitch with the main color. Drop both stitches off. Place the resulting stitch onto the left needle, knit the second stitch through the back loop with the main color, then knit the first stitch with the contrast color. Drop both stitches off. Place the resulting stitch onto the left needle. Repeat from *, alternating the contrast color and main color (figure 4). End as for the one-color method to get back to the required stitch

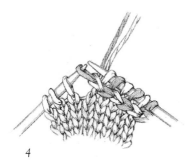

4

Two-color vikkel braid.

count. *Tip:* The color you use when you knit into the back of the stitch is the same color as the stitch just transferred. Then knit into the transferred stitch with the other color.

Three-color: In this technique, the braid is made up of two contrast colors and the stitches on the needle are made up of the main color (figure 5). Work as above, beginning with one of the contrast colors. After placing the first stitch back to the left needle, knit the second stitch through the back loop with the main color and knit into the first stitch with the other contrast color. Drop both stitches off. Continue in this manner, working the second stitch through the back loop first with the main color and then alternating contrast colors for the first stitch (the second stitch worked).

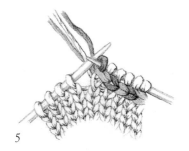

5

Two-color vikkel braid.

Contrast-color: Work as for the three-color braid, beginning by increasing one stitch with the contrast color. Place this stitch back onto the left needle, knit the second stitch through the back loop with the main color, then knit the first stitch with the contrast color. Drop both stitches off. Continue in this manner, knitting the second stitch through the back loop with the main color and then knitting the first stitch with the contrast color (figure 6).

6

Contrast-color vikkel braid.

Kihnu vits

This type of braid comes from Kihnu. In Estonian, *vits* describes the bands that encircle wooden beer mugs, made like a cooper's barrel. In this case, the band encircles the cuff of a mitten or the leg of a sock.

Knit one round alternating a contrast yarn with the main color. On the next round, bring both yarns to the front as if to purl, *purl the contrast-color stitch

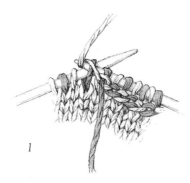

1

Kihnu vits braid.

with the main color (figure 1), purl the main-color stitch with the contrast color. Repeat from *, bringing the new color *under* the old every time you change.

Three-color twist

I've seen this twisted rope-like decoration on several knitted pieces from Estonia worked with two or more colors. The following instructions are for three colors of yarn.

*With colors 2 and 3 forward, knit one stitch with color 1, then bring this color forward and let it drop. Bring color 2 under colors 3 and 1 and to the back, then use it to knit the next stitch (figure 1). Bring this yarn forward and let it drop. Bring color 3 under colors 1 and 2 and to the back, then use it to knit the next stitch (figure 2). Bring this yarn froward and let it drop. Repeat from *, always bringing the next color *under* the last two used.

Roositud Inlay

Roos is the Estonian word for rose. Roositud is an inlay technique that allows color to be worked in specific places without carrying the contrast color(s) all around the circumference of a piece. To me, this type of color work appears like a garden of flowers

This technique is worked following a charted pattern. You may find it helpful to arrange the stitches so that all the stitches involved in a motif are on the same needle. Use double or (my preference) thicker yarn for the inlay pattern.

Work across the first pattern row, laying in the colors as indicated on the roositud chart. Leave the pattern yarn to the left of the pattern area as you complete the round with the main color (figure 1). On the next round, knit to where you need the pattern yarn, lift up the pattern yarn and bring it to the front of the work, over the top of the left needle, leaving a loop (figure 2). Place the loose end of the pattern yarn

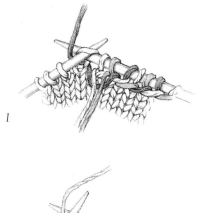

1

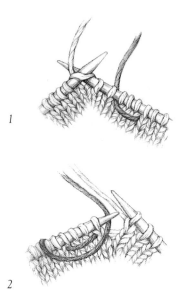

1

2

Three-color twist.

2

Roositud inlay.

behind the work between the needles at the point indicated by the chart (figure 3). As you work across the pattern area with the main color, bring the loop forward or backward as needed (figure 4), to place the pattern yarn as necessary. When you have completed the inlay, tug on the loose end of the pattern yarn to tighten it up (figure 5). The end of the pattern yarn is now back at the right side of the pattern area, ready to begin again on the next round.

call a clock. I believe this patterning was just used for decorative clocks on stockings and traveled, as many good pattern ideas do, on to other types of knitted garments, particularly gloves.

Left-to-right slant

Knit two stitches together (figure 1), knit the first stitch again (figure 2), then slip both stitches off the needle (figure 3).

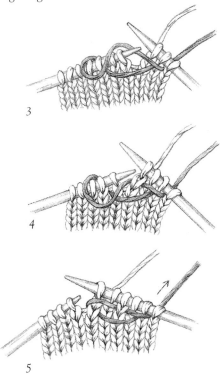

Roositud inlay.

Vikkel Stitches

Made up of diagonal lines, vikkel patterns form zigzags and diamonds. I surmise that this word has something to do with *Zwickle*, the German term for the wedge shape at the ankle of a stocking—what we

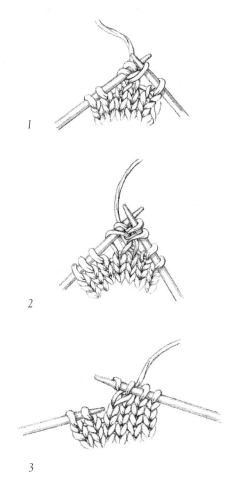

Left-to-right vikkel stitch.

Right-to-left slant

Pass the right needle behind the first stitch on the left needle, knit the second stitch through the back loop (figure 1), knit the first stitch as usual (figure 2), then slip both stitches off the needle (figure 3).

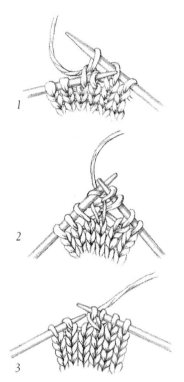

Right-to-left vikkel stitch.

Thumb Opening

Estonians typically work gusset-less thumbs, also known as "peasant" or "stocking" thumbs. The opening is marked by working the required number of stitches with contrasting waste yarn (choose a smooth, slick cotton yarn in a bright, contrasting color).

Work to where the thumb opening will begin. With waste yarn, knit across the specified number of thumb stitches. Now slip the stitches you just knit back onto the left needle and work across them in the established pattern (making these stitches one row longer than the rest of the mitten; figure 1), and work to the end of the round in the established pattern. When you are ready

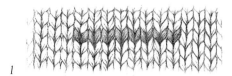

Thumb stitches "held" on waste yarn.

to work the thumb, remove the waste yarn and place the resulting stitches onto double-pointed needles. There will be the same number of stitches you worked across on the front or lower row, and one less stitch on the back or upper row. I find it easiest to pick up these stitches by placing the stitches onto needles before pulling out the waste yarn (figure 2). If I need the same number of stitches on both rows, that is, an extra stitch on the back row, I simply pick up one extra stitch between the front and back stitches and place it on the back needle, making sure not to twist the stitch.

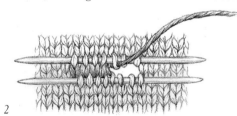

When you're ready to work thumb, place held stitches onto two double-pointed needles, then onto three or four for knitting.

Nupp Stitch

Nupp has been translated for me as "button." My Estonian/English dictionary also tells me it means bud. I rather like the idea of a bud stitch, because buds are flowers to be, and my thoughts of Estonia always involve flowers.

Bring the right needle in front of the first two stitches and under the left needle between the second and third stitch. Wrap the working yarn clockwise (opposite of usual wrap) around the right needle (figure 1) and draw a loop through. Now wrap the working yarn around right needle clockwise (figure 2), draw this wrap through the loop (figure 3), and tighten yarn. Place the right needle into the two wrapped stitches and slip them onto the right needle (figure 4). Pass the new stitch over the top of these two stitches and off the needle (figure 5).

Heart of a blossom

This well-known technique is used for finishing toes of socks, tips of fingers and thumbs, and tops of mittens. In Estonian, it is called *õie süda*, which translates to "heart of a blossom." I was so enchanted with this term that when I first learned it, I decided then and there that it would be my finish of choice for ever more. For me, it works best with about eight stitches—fewer than six stitches results in a pointy tip, more than eight, a bulky one.

Break the working yarn, leaving a tail about eight inches (20.5 cm) long. Thread the tail on a darning needle, run the needle through each live stitch as you drop it off the knitting needle (figure 1), then pull to tighten (figure 2). Weave the yarn end into the inside of the piece, securely and neatly.

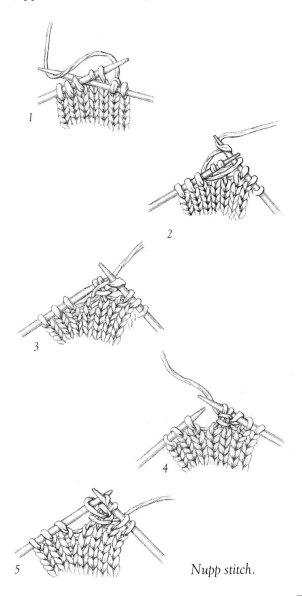

Nupp stitch.

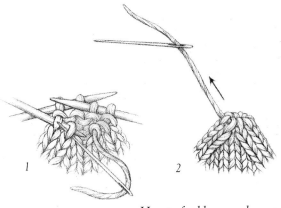

Heart of a blossom closure.

THE DESIGNS

Choosing the designs for this book was one of the most difficult, yet most enjoyable experiences of my knitting life. I had so much to choose from and to be inspired by, and yet I knew I needed to think of you, the knitter, and what you like to make. Then I had to blend your desires with my goal of recording the historic and traditional aspects of this wonderful knitting legacy.

Nine of the patterns are what I hope are close reproductions of older knitted works. These include Meida's Mittens, Hilja's Mittens, Marko's Mittens, Liivi's Stockings, Avo's Mittens, Kalev's Mittens, Virve's Stockings, Liidia's Gloves, and Helgi's Mittens. All were taken from knitting I studied in a museum, from my own slides, or from reproductions in texts about Estonian knitting. In some cases the originals were made of finer yarn at a tighter gauge with more pattern repeats. Adjusting for the yarn I was using, I achieved as close a match as possible.

The other patterns offered here have all been inspired by Estonian knitting—traditional and/or contemporary pieces. I've changed patterns to offer an overview of motifs, trying all the while to keep the feel and spirit of Estonian knitting in every piece. In some cases I've changed colors—I'm sure the original purple on Kristi's Mittens wasn't so bold. In other cases I've varied an idea for today's knitters. Landra's Gloves don't include the back-of-hand patterning that was on the originals, and the roositud pieces (Aino's Gloves, Anu's Stockings and Ulla's Gloves) are done with yarn heavier than the originals, therefore with less detailed patterning. Since I was using a heavier yarn for the color work, I had to eliminate the colored yarn knitted into the piece, making a need for changes in how the patterns were worked from the originals.

Some of the pieces were inspired by modern ones knitted in the last year or so, available in Estonian markets or shops, or given as gifts. Examples of these are Anu's Christmas Gloves, Ilmar's Socks, Rita's Stockings, Merike's Gloves, Maarja's Socks, Ellen's Socks, Juta's Stockings, Laila's Socks, and Tiit's Socks. For these projects I've changed patterns or colors and added small details to make the pattern work my way. As a designer, I find it difficult not to let inspiration and curiosity propel me through a design, but I always feel close to the Estonian knitters, past and present, who have made the projects possible. Their knitting is very alive, ever-changing, and it seems they are always trying new techniques and putting patterns together in new ways. They are constantly learning and adapting, while keeping the general feeling of their heritage. Over the past years, I have tried to touch the Estonian soul, at least in knitting, though I will never truly understand it all. I hope I have achieved at least some of this balance in these pieces.

The remaining designs in the book are ones I invented, inspired by traditional patterns or ones I enjoy. Anu's Mittens are taken from gloves in the same pattern. I changed the cuff pattern a bit, and made mittens because the glove gauge called for a finer yarn than I had available. Maimu's mittens are also an invention. I wanted to use more braids and the nupp stitch, so I put them together in the cuff. For the hand I chose the

Elk Horn pattern, a cross pattern set in a grid. Sander's Mittens were inspired by gloves with the Cat's Paw pattern; I substituted colors I enjoy for the original red and yellow.

In the process of researching this book, I discovered a wealth of interesting Estonian techniques I hadn't known about. Many that I enjoyed working out and looking at are all offered here. One of my challenges was to find a way to use all these techniques in the projects. I have done that, if only once in some cases. So, if you knit every project, you'll have a chance to learn every Estonian technique offered.

Socks or stockings, mittens and the more elaborate gloves, all make interesting small projects. There is nothing more comfortable—and comforting—than a well-fitting pair of wool gloves, mittens, or socks on a wintry day. Circular knitting has lent itself best to these small garments, ones that need to fit snugly and cover the unique shapes of hand and foot.

If this is the first time you've knitted socks, mittens, or gloves, the best way to begin is to make a pair that is plain, in a good wool. It is the thumb and, of course, fingers for gloves, that is the challenge for hand coverings; turning the heel is the real magic in making a sock.

All the socks and stockings in this book have a square or Dutch heel. This shaping appears quite often in sock-knitting instructions, and seems to be the one most widely used in Estonia. This said, I have seen Estonian socks with other heel shapings, some very inventive. I chose this shaping because it is universal in Estonia.

All the mittens in this book have what I call a stocking thumb, the most typical for Estonian mittens. This is a simple thumb with the opening worked from the palm with no gusset at the thumb base. While stocking thumbs may not have refinements in shaping, they are a pleasure to work and allow for fun stuff in the patterning, from having it grow out of the hand pattern

(Marko's Mittens) to a complete change in the pattern (Helgi's Mittens).

All the gloves but Merike's have this style of thumb. It is really the fingers of gloves that are fun. Fingers are small technical wonders and quite satisfying to make. You'll achieve a better fit if you start the little finger before the others—about ¼ of an inch is a good spacing. This is done on Landra's Gloves, Merike's Gloves, and Ulla's Gloves only, as many of the Estonian gloves I have studied began all the fingers at the same height. Finger stitches are determined by dividing the amount you have for the hand into four and then adding one or two stitches to the index finger and/or other fingers, while subtracting the same number from the little finger. Cast on stitches at the base of each finger to join each group of stitches into a round. When you work the next finger, pick up stitches into these cast-on stitches to create a fourchette. If you pick up two more stitches than were cast on between fingers, you can work a decrease at either side of the picked-up stitches to close up any holes that have occurred between fingers. Decreases in these patterns are a sl 1, k1, psso at the beginning of the group of stitches and a k2tog at the end. I like this method of creating fingers because the small gussets at each side allow for better finger movement and a tidier finish.

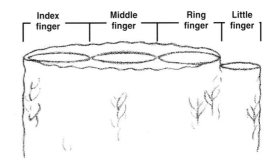

Begin the little finger on gloves about ¼" before the other fingers. Shown here is palm side of left hand.

I've written all the instructions keyed to needle position. The round always begins with needle #1 and ends with needle #4, but where that break is placed depends on what you're knitting. For mittens and gloves, the beginning of the round is placed along the outside of the hand where it is less noticeable. For socks and stockings, the beginning of the round usually runs along the back of the leg.

Decreasing the top of thumb and fingers down to about eight stitches gives a better look than decreasing to less. These patterns offer two ways to decrease—in a wedge by decreasing at both sides of the mitten top, the glove fingers, and thumb, or by shaping a circular decrease, alternating decrease and plain rounds. These decreases all end in the heart of a blossom finish, an especially picturesque title for a very simple closure.

When you're knitting socks, stockings, mittens, or gloves, take the recipient's measurements into account. Foot length and width is an important factor, as are hand width and finger length. Make adjustments to the patterns where necessary to achieve the fit you desire.

I finished each pair of mittens, socks, and gloves by wet blocking them. First I washed them in warm water with a little soap, rinsed them, then let them air dry on blockers. I used wooden sock and mitten blockers when possible and made blockers from cardboard when I needed a different shape, such as pointed mitten or thumb tops. Blocking fingers required cutting out a heavy cardboard shape, which seems to work just fine; the cardboard holds up even when damp. You can also steam block with a damp cloth over the piece, using just the heat of the iron, not its pressure, to set the shape. I find that blocking really makes knitted fabric look wonderful, so don't pass up the opportunity to do it!

What about storing your wonderful handknitted, woolen treasures? My Estonian friend Rita tells me that she stores her woolen treasures in newspaper! I assume that moths and other wool-eating creatures don't like the ink. To prevent ink stains, I recommend first wrapping the items in plain paper or tissue paper—acid free would be really good.

ABBREVIATIONS

beg	beginning; begin; begins	k	knit	rib	ribbing
bet	between	k2tog	knit two stitches together	rnd(s)	round(s)
BO	bind off	m	marker	sl	slip
CC	contrast color	MC	main color	st(s)	stitch(es)
cm	centimeter(s)	mm	millimeter(s)	St st	stockinette stitch
CO	cast on	p	purl	tbl	through back loop
cont	continue; continuing	p2tog	purl two stitches together	tog	together
dec(s)	decrease(s); decreasing	patt(s)	pattern(s)	yo	yarn over
dpn	double-pointed needle(s)	pm	place marker	*	repeat starting point (i.e., repeat from *)
foll	following	psso	pass slipped stitch over		
g	gram(s)	rem	remain; remaining		
inc(s)	increase(s); increasing	rep	repeat		

AINO'S GLOVES

*T*hese decorative gloves were inspired by a glove pictured in Konsin's book, Slimkoeesemed, from Tori, a village northeast of Pärnu. They are named for Aino Pödra, the knitter who taught me the method of the double-start cast-on, used here, and also how to do the Roositud inlay pattern in a most logical way. I love Roositud pattern because it can be placed anywhere and comprise many colors. This glove has a cuff very like the original, with patterning on the little finger, middle finger, back of hand, and thumb. The originals of these types of gloves were knitted in finer yarn, resulting in a much finer gauge and giving great opportunity for more detail in the patterning. The inlay yarn is usually a double strand of the knitting yarn or a thicker yarn of the same type, as used here.

Yarn: Rauma Finullgarn (100% wool; 180 yd [165 m]/50 g): #401 natural (MC), 2 skeins; Rauma Strikkegarn (100% wool; 115 yd [105 m]/50 g) #144 red (CC1) and #7/61 green, small amount of each. Small amount of contrasting waste yarn.

Needles: Size 00 (1.75 mm): Set of 5 double-pointed.

Gauge: 17 sts and 26 rnds = 2" (5 cm) in St st. Adjust needle size if necessary to obtain the correct gauge.

Finished size: To fit a woman's hand: about 9" (23 cm) around and 8" (20.5 cm) long, excluding cuff.

LEFT GLOVE

Cuff: With natural and using the double-start method with 2 yarns over the thumb (see page 42), CO 72 sts. Divide sts evenly onto 4 dpn (18 sts each needle). Using the crossover method (see page 46), join, being careful not to twist sts. Knit 1 rnd. Purl 1 rnd. Knit 2 rnds. Purl 1 rnd. Knit 3 rnds. Purl 1 rnd. Knit 7 rnds. Purl 1 rnd. *Next rnd:* *YO, k2tog; rep from *. Purl 1 rnd. Knit 14 rnds. Purl 1 rnd. Knit 1 rnd, inc 6 sts evenly spaced —78 sts. Arrange sts so that there are 20 sts each on needles #2 and #3, and 19 sts each on needles #1 and #4.

Hand: Work 39 sts on needles #1 and #2 (palm sts). Beg with Row 1, and foll directions on chart, beg Roositud inlay (see page 52) as indicated (the finger chart is worked on last 8 sts on needle #4; the back-of-hand chart begs on 14th st on needle #3 on Row 13). Work as charted until piece measures 1½" (3.8 cm) from top of cuff (about 17 rnds), or to desired length to thumb opening. **Mark thumb opening:** (Row 24 of chart) K21, k16 with waste yarn, sl these 16 sts back onto left needle, work to end in established patt. Cont in patt until 54 rows of inlay have been worked or piece measures 1¾" (4.5 cm) from thumb waste yarn, or desired length to base of little finger. **Little finger:** Place last 9 sts on needle #4 onto 1 dpn and first 9 sts on needle #1 onto another dpn for finger. Place rem 60 hand sts onto a length of yarn until needed. K9 palm sts, using the backward loop method (see page 45) CO 6 sts, k9 back-of-hand sts in patt—24 finger sts. Arrange finger sts evenly onto 4 dpn (6 sts each needle) and join into a rnd. Cont patt as established to second-to-last patt rnd or until piece measures to middle of fingernail (about ¾" [2 cm] less than desired total length). **Shape top:** With natural, work a 3-part spiral as foll:
Rnd 1: *K6, k2tog; rep from *—21 sts rem.

Rnd 2: *K5, k2tog; rep from *—18 sts rem.
Rnd 3: *K4, k2tog; rep from *—15 sts rem.

Cont dec in this manner until 9 sts rem. Finish off with a heart of a blossom closure (see page 55). **Ring finger:** Place the next 9 sts on each side of the hand onto dpn. Join natural at left of little finger and work across 9 palm sts, CO 6 sts, work across 9 back-of-hand sts, pick up and knit 6 sts along 6 cast-on sts at base of little finger—30 sts total. Arrange sts evenly onto 4 dpn. Work in St st until finger measures to middle of fingernail (about ¾" [2 cm] less than total desired length). **Shape top:**
Rnd 1: *K8, k2tog; rep from *—27 sts rem.
Rnd 2: *K7, k2tog; rep from *—24 sts rem.
Rnd 3: *K6, k2tog; rep from *—21 sts rem.

Cont dec in this manner until 9 sts rem. Finish off with a heart of a blossom closure. **Middle finger:** Work as for ring finger, joining yarn at base of ring finger and picking up and knitting sts at base of ring finger—30 sts total. Work patt as charted, shape top as for ring finger. **Index finger:** Place 24 rem sts onto dpn. Join natural at the base of the middle finger, k24, pick up and knit 6 sts at base of middle finger—30 sts total. Work as for ring finger. **Thumb:** Remove waste yarn, place 16 front sts onto 2 dpn, 15 back sts onto 2 other dpn, and pick up 1 st at one end of back sts—32 sts. Join yarn at right side of opening, pick up and knit 1 st, k16, pick up and knit 1 st, k16—34 sts. *Next rnd:* Sl 1, k1, psso, beg inlay patt as charted, k2tog at beg of back sts, work to end—32 sts rem (8 sts each needle). Work thumb as charted until piece measures to middle of thumbnail (about ¾" [2 cm] less than desired total length). **Shape top:**
Rnd 1: K8, k2tog, [k9, k2tog] 2 times—29 sts rem.
Rnd 2: K7, k2tog, [k8, k2tog] 2 times—26 sts rem.
Rnd 3: K6, k2tog, [k7, k2tog] 2 times—23 sts rem.

Cont dec in this manner until 8 sts rem. Finish off with a heart of a blossom closure. Weave in loose ends. Block.

RIGHT GLOVE

Work cuff and cont in back-of-hand patt, beg Roositud inlay as indicated (the finger inlay is worked on first 8 sts on needle #1; the back-of-hand inlay begs on 5th st on needle #2 on Row 13). Work to thumb opening as for left glove, working back-of-hand sts on needles #1 and #2, and palm sts on needles #3 and #4. **Mark thumb opening:** Work 41 sts in patt, k16 with waste yarn, sl these 16 sts back onto left needle, knit to end. Cont as for left glove.

Aino's finger

red ●
green ×
natural □

Aino's back of hand

← Mark thumb opening

D C   B A

Left glove: Rows 1-12: Work palm sts on needles #1 and 2,
work to last 9 sts on needle #4, work 9-st little finger pattern.
Begin back-of-hand pattern on Row 13 at B (needle #3), end at
D, work 9-st little finger pattern.
Right glove: Rows 1-12: Work 9-st little finger pattern on needle #1, knit to end. Begin back-of-hand pattern on Row 13 at A
(needle #1), end at C, work palm sts.

Middle finger pattern

Little finger pattern

Thumb pattern

ANU'S CHRISTMAS GLOVES

*T*hese fanciful gloves were inspired by a pair my dear friend, Anu Kaljurand, received from her parents for Christmas when she was studying in Utah. They are a fine example of the wonderful surprises found in Estonian knitting. The top of the hand is fun and interesting—turn the hand over and the shock of stripes will make you smile! They begin with a double-start cast-on, followed right away by a two-color vikkel braid. After a bit more knitting, another vikkel braid is worked.

Yarn: Tuna (100% wool; 350 yd [320 m]/100 g) #3001 sheep's white (MC), #3730 dark gray, 1 skein each. Small amount of contrasting waste yarn.

Needles: Size 1 (2.25 mm): Set of 5 double-pointed.

Gauge: 15 sts and 18 rnds = 2" (5 cm) in snowflake patt; 17 sts and 17 rnds = 2" (5 cm) in palm patt.

Finished size: To fit a woman's hand: about 7½" (19 cm) around and 6¾" (17 cm) long, excluding cuff. Adjust needle size if necessary to obtain the correct gauge.

LEFT GLOVE

Cuff: With dark gray and using the double-start method with 2 yarns over the thumb (see page 42), CO 50 sts. Divide sts evenly onto 4 dpn (12 sts each on needles #1 and #3, 13 sts each on needles #2 and #4). Using the crossover method (see page 46), join, being careful not to twist sts. Work Rows 1–26 of cuff chart.

Hand: With sheep's white, work 4 rnds St st, inc 1 st at beg of needle #3 and end of needle #4, and 5 sts evenly spaced across needles #1 and #2 (palm sts)—57 sts total; 27 back-of-hand sts and 30 palm sts. K2 gray, [k2 sheep's white, k2 gray] 7 times, beg with Row 1, work back-of-hand chart (be sure to catch in the long gray floats while working patt, and take care not to knit too tightly). Cont striped patt on palm sts, work through Row 12 of back-of-hand chart or desired length to thumb opening. ***Mark thumb opening:*** (Row 13 of chart) K15 in patt, k14 with waste yarn, sl these 14 sts back onto left needle, work to end in patt. Cont in established patt to Row 28 of chart or until piece measures 1¾" (4.5 cm) from thumb waste yarn, or desired length to base of little finger. ***Little finger:*** Place the last 7 sts on needle #4 onto 1 dpn and the first 9 sts on needle #1 onto another dpn for finger. Place rem 41 hand sts onto a length of yarn until needed. K9 palm sts, using the backward loop method (see page 45) CO 5 sts as foll: CO 1 gray, 2 white, 2 gray, k7 back-of-hand sts as charted—21 sts. Arrange finger sts evenly onto 4 dpn and join into a rnd. Work in established patt until piece measures to middle of fingernail (about ¾" [2 cm] less than desired total length). *Shape top:* Cut sheep's white.

Rnds 1, 2, and 4: Knit.

Rnd 3: *K1, k2tog; rep from *—14 sts rem.

Rnd 5: *K2tog; rep from *—7 sts rem.

Finish off with a heart of a blossom closure (see page 55).

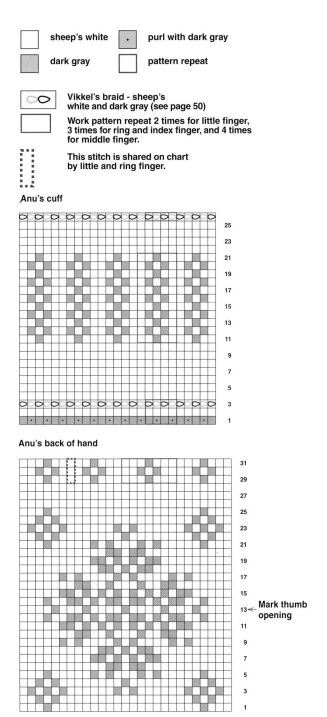

sheep's white

· purl with dark gray

dark gray

pattern repeat

Vikkel's braid - sheep's white and dark gray (see page 50)

Work pattern repeat 2 times for little finger, 3 times for ring and index finger, and 4 times for middle finger.

This stitch is shared on chart by little and ring finger.

Anu's cuff

Anu's back of hand

13 ← Mark thumb opening

Ring finger: Place the next 7 palm sts and 6 back-of-hand sts onto dpn. Join yarns at base of little finger (palm facing) and work across palm sts as established, CO 6 sts in patt, work across 6 back-of-hand sts, pick up 1 sheep's white st (this st is shared by the ring and little fingers), pick up and knit 5 sts in stripe patt at base of little finger—25 sts total. Arrange sts evenly onto 4 dpn and join into a rnd. Work in patt until piece measures to middle of fingernail (about ¾" [2 cm] less than desired total length). *Shape top:* Cut sheep's white.

Rnds 1, 2, and 4: Knit.
Rnd 3: *K1, k2tog; rep from *, end k1—17 sts rem.
Rnd 5: *K2tog; rep from *, end k1—9 sts rem.

Finish off with a heart of a blossom closure. *Middle finger:* Join yarn at base of ring finger and work as for ring finger (omitting shared st). *Index finger:* Place 16 rem sts onto dpn. Join sheep's white at base of middle finger, work across all sts in established patt, pick up and knit 5 sts in patt at base of middle finger—21 sts total. Work in patt until piece measures to middle of fingernail (about ¾" [2 cm] less than desired total length). Shape top as for little finger. *Thumb:* Remove waste yarn, place 14 front sts onto 2 dpn, 13 back sts onto 2 other dpn, and pick up 1 st at one end of back sts—28 sts total. Join yarn at right side of opening. Pick up and knit 1 st with the same color as the next st, k14 in striped patt, pick up and knit 1 st with the same color as the next st, k14 in striped patt—30 sts. Arrange sts evenly onto 4 dpn and join into a rnd. *Next rnd:* K2tog, work 14 front sts in patt, k2tog, work to end of rnd—28 sts total. Cont in striped patt until piece measures to middle of thumbnail (about ¾" [2 cm] less than desired total length). *Shape top:* Cut sheep's white.

Rnds 1, 2, and 4: Knit.
Rnd 3: *K1, k2tog; rep from *, end k1—19 sts rem.
Rnd 5: *K2tog; rep from *, end k1—10 sts rem.

Finish off with a heart of a blossom closure. Weave in loose ends. Block.

RIGHT GLOVE

Work cuff and cont in patt to thumb opening as for left glove, working 27 back-of-hand sts on needles #1 and #2, and 30 palm sts on needles #3 and #4. *Mark thumb opening:* (Row 13 of chart) K28 in patt, k14 with waste yarn, sl these 14 sts back onto left needle, knit to end in patt. Work hand, fingers, and thumb as for left glove.

Anv's Mittens

Yarn: Satakieli (100% wool; 360 yd [330 m]/100 g): #462 red, #003 natural, 1 skein each; #890 green, partial skein. Small amount of contrasting waste yarn.
Needles: Size 0 (2 mm): Set of 5 double-pointed.
Gauge: 18 sts and 22 rnds = 2" (5 cm) in color patt. Adjust needle size if necessary to obtain the correct gauge.
Finished size: To fit a woman's hand; about 8" (20.5 cm) around and 8" (20.5 cm) long, excluding cuff.

Cuff: With red and using the Continental method, (see page 41) CO 72 sts. Divide sts evenly onto 4 dpn (18 sts each needle). Using the crossover method (see page 46), join, being careful not to twist sts. Beg with Row 1, work to end of cuff chart (note that there will be 68 sts after Row 2), inc 1 st at the end of each needle on last rnd—72 sts (18 sts each needle).

Hand: Work Rows 1–12 of hand and thumb chart 2 times, then Rows 1–6—piece should measure about 2½" (6.5 cm) from top of cuff, or desired length to thumb opening, ending with Row 6 or 12 of chart. **Mark thumb opening:** *Left mitten:* K20 in patt, k15 with waste yarn, sl these 15 sts back onto left needle, knit to end in patt; *Right mitten:* K38 in patt, k15 with waste yarn, sl these 15 sts back onto left needle, knit to end in patt. Cont in patt until piece measures to top of little finger (about 1½" [3.8 cm] less than desired total length), ending with Row 6 or 12 of chart. **Shape top:** With red and using the one-wick method (see page 47), work double-dec on last st of needle #4 and first 2 sts on needle #1, and again on last st on needle #2 and first 2 sts on needle #3—4 sts dec'd. Working patt as established, dec in this manner every rnd until 8 sts rem, and *at the same time,* after working 12 rows of chart, work all but dec sts in natural only. Finish off with a heart of a blossom closure (see page 55). **Thumb:** Remove waste yarn and place 15 front sts on needles #1 and #2, and 14 back sts on needles #3 and #4. Join natural at right side of opening, pick up and knit 1 st with natural, k15 front sts, pick up and knit 1 st, join red, work 14 back sts in patt—31 sts total. On the next rnd, cont in patt, knitting the last st on needle #4 tog with the first st on needle #1—30 sts rem; 15 front sts on

Anu's Mittens

These ladies' mittens were inspired by gloves from the village of Paistu, in Viljandimaa. They are named for Anu Raud, an honored Estonian crafts woman, weaver of exquisite tapestries, and collector of the folk art of her people. Anu raises the sheep for her wool, lives surrounded by woodland and field, near Paistu, and works tirelessly to keep alive the traditions she loves so much.

She teaches adults and children about their culture and makes Estonian heritage available to visitors at the Heimtali Museum near her home.

A Continental cast-on begins the cuff, which is shaped with decreases and increases. A six-stitch pattern repeat follows for the hand and thumb. Both finish with a one-wick decrease.

needles #1 and #2, and 15 back sts on needles #3 and #4. Cont in patt until piece measures to middle of thumbnail (about ¾" [2 cm] less than desired total length), ending with Row 6 or 12 of chart. *Shape top:* Cut natural. Using the one-wick method and red, work double-decs as for mitten top until 6 sts rem. Finish off with a heart of a blossom closure. Weave in loose ends. Block.

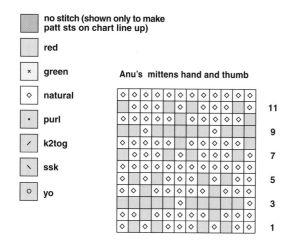

no stitch (shown only to make patt sts on chart line up)

red

× **green**

◇ **natural**

• **purl**

╱ **k2tog**

╲ **ssk**

○ **yo**

Anu's mittens hand and thumb

Anu's mittens cuff

Anu's Stockings

Yarn: Rauma Finullgarn (100% wool; 180 yd [165 m]/50 g): #401 natural (MC), 3 skeins. Rauma Strikkegarn (100% wool; 115 yd [105 m]/50 g): #144 red and #147 blue, partial skein each.

Needles: Size 0 (2 mm): Set 5 double-pointed (dpn).

Gauge: 16 sts and 24 rnds = 2" (5 cm) in St st. Adjust needle size if necessary to obtain the correct gauge.

Finished size: To fit a woman's foot: About 8½" (21.5 cm) around and 9¼" (23.5 cm) long.

Note: You may find it easier to work the roositud with all the stitches on one needle. Then arrange the stitches on four needles as specified before beginning the heel and gussets.

Leg: With MC and using the Continental method (see page 41), CO 88 sts. Divide sts onto 4 dpn with 26 sts each on needles #1 and #4, and 18 sts each on needles #2 and #3. This arrangement of sts is very important as you work the stocking. Using the crossover method (see page 46), join, being careful not to twist sts. Work k2, p2 ribbing for 15 rnds—piece should measure about 1" (2.5 cm) from beg. Work 12 rnds in St st. Beg seam chart at back of leg, centered over the first 3 and last 3 sts of the rnd. (To help work the seam patt, move the last 2 sts of the rnd onto needle #1 so that the purl st at the right edge of the seam patt—the first st on the chart—is the last st on needle #4.) Cont as established until piece measures 5" (12.5 cm) from beg. *Shape leg:* Work 5 sts in patt, sl 1, k1, psso, work to last 3 sts, k2tog, p1. Dec 1 st each side of seam patt in this manner every 9 rnds 8 times total—72 sts rem. *At the same time,* when piece measures 6" (15 cm) from beg, begin roositud (see page 52) "clocks" along each side of stocking so that the center sts of the patt are the first st on needle #2 and the last st on needle #3. Work Rows 1–26 of chart 3 times total—6 stars along each side; piece should measure about 11½" (29 cm) from beg or desired length to beg of heel.

Heel: Place the 2 sts you moved from needle #4 onto needle #1 back onto needle #4 (so that the seam patt is centered over the heel). Discontinue working the seam patt. *Heel flap:* K18, turn. Sl 1, p35. These 36 sts will form the heel flap; the

ANU'S STOCKINGS

This very traditional pair of stockings is named for Anu Liivandi, the registrar at the Royal Ontario Museum in Toronto. She was the first Estonian I ever met and she helped me in many ways, not only by arranging access to the ROM's collection of Estonian knitting, but with advice and support about many things Estonian. I named these stockings for her because the museum has a pair something like them that I was fortunate enough to study in detail. Several different styles of stockings were done with roositud inlay down the leg as "clocks." The historic ones were done in much finer yarn, with the pattern yarn being double or simply thicker. The color scheme, where the red and blue alternate, is very typical. A Continental cast-on is used for this stocking.

rem 36 sts will form the instep. Slipping the first st of every row will create chain sts at each edge.

Row 1: (RS) Sl 1, k35.

Row 2: Sl 1, p35.

Rep Rows 1 and 2 for a total of 36 rows, ending with Row 2 (18 chain sts each edge). **Turn heel:**

Row 1: (RS) K23, sl 1, k1, psso.

Row 2: Sl 1, p10, p2tog.

Row 3: Sl 1, k10, sl 1, k1, psso.

Rep Rows 2 and 3 until all the waiting sts have been used, ending with Row 2—12 heel sts rem.

Foot: (RS) K12 heel sts and with the same needle, pick up and knit 18 sts along left side of heel flap; with 2 other needles, work across 36 held instep sts, cont to work half the roositud patt at the beg of needle #2 and end of needle #3; with rem needle, pick up and knit 18 sts along right side of heel flap, and k6 heel sts—84 sts total; 24 left heel and gusset sts on needle #1, 18 instep sts each on needles #2 and #3, and 24 right heel and gusset sts on needle #4. Rnd begs at back of heel. **Shape gusset:** Cont working half of roositud patt at beg of needle #2 and end of needle #3 as charted.

Rnd 1: Work to last 3 sts on needle #1, k2tog, k1, k36, k1, sl 1, k1, psso, work to end.

Rnd 2: Work even.

Cont to dec 2 sts every other rnd in this manner 6 times total—72 sts rem; 18 sts each needle. After three partial roositud stars have been worked, cont even in St st until foot measures about 2¾" (7 cm) less than desired total length. **Shape toe:**

Rnd 1: *Knit to last 2 sts on needle, k2tog; rep from * to end of rnd—4 sts dec'd.

Rnd 2: Knit.

Rep Rnd 1 and 2 a total of 6 times—48 sts rem; 12 sts each needle. Then work Rnd 1 only until 8 sts rem—2 sts each needle. Finish off with a heart of a blossom closure (see page 55). Weave in loose ends. Block.

Anu's leg and foot

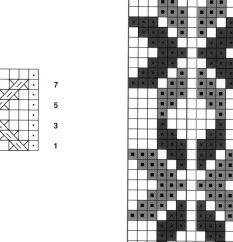

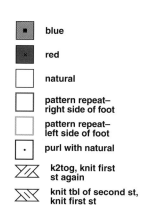

	blue
	red
	natural
	pattern repeat– right side of foot
	pattern repeat– left side of foot
·	purl with natural
	k2tog, knit first st again
	knit tbl of second st, knit first st

Leg: Repeat Rows 1-26 three times.
Foot: Repeat purple highlighted area 1½ times for right side of foot and blue highlighted area for left side of foot.

Avo's Mittens

Avo Pödra is the kind and cheerful husband of Aino, and father to Leila. He told me a story of the knitters on one of the islands getting together in the evenings to knit. They did this to have company but also, perhaps more importantly, to save on precious lamp oil. Avo also was the driver of a wonderful Suzuki mini van, which was the "magic carpet" on which I visited Muhu and Saaremaa one chilly spring weekend.

This mitten was inspired by one pictured in Mulgi Kirikindad ja Kirisukad. It is worked in a pattern that has two different names from two different areas: Põrnikakiri or bug pattern from Väike-Määrja, or Sookiri or bog or marsh pattern from Helme.

The ribbed cuff begins with a Continental cast-on. The top of the mitten and the thumb are shaped with two-color, two-wick decreases.

Yarn: Tuna (100% wool; 350 yd [320 m]/100 g): #3730 dark gray and #3001 natural, 1 skein each. Small amount of contrasting waste yarn.

Needles: Size 0 (2 mm) and size 1 (2.25 mm): Set of 5 double-pointed each.

Gauge: 18 sts and 18 rnds = 2" (5 cm) in color patt on larger needles. Adjust needle sizes if necessary to obtain the correct gauge.

Finished size: To fit a man's hand; about 8½" (21.5 cm) around and 8" (20.5 cm) long, excluding cuff.

Cuff: With gray, smaller needles, and using the Continental method (see page 41), CO 76 sts. Divide sts evenly onto 4 dpn (19 sts each needle). Using the crossover method (see page 46), join, being careful not to twist sts.

Rnds 1–4, 10–11, 16–23, 29–31, and 37–40: With gray, *k2, p2; rep from *.

Rnds 5, 12, 24, and 32: With natural, knit.

Rnds 6–8, 13–15, 25–27, and 33–35: With natural, *k2, p2; rep from *.

Rnds 9, 17, 28, and 36: With gray, knit.

Rnd 41: With gray, knit, inc 2 sts evenly spaced—78 sts; 19 sts each on needles #1 and #4, 20 sts each on needles #2 and #3.

Hand: Change to larger dpn and rep Rows 1–8 of hand chart for a total of 22 rows—piece should measure about 2½" (6.5 cm) from top of cuff, or desired length to thumb opening, ending with Row 2 or 6 of chart. **Mark thumb opening:** *Left mitten:* K21 in patt, k16 with waste yarn, sl these 16 sts back onto left needle, knit to end in patt; *Right mitten:* K41 in patt,

k16 with waste yarn, sl these 16 sts back onto left needle, knit to end in patt. Cont in patt until piece measures to top of little finger (about 2" [5 cm] less than desired total length). **Shape top:** Using the two-wick method (see page 48) and alternating gray and natural for the dec working yarn, work double-decs as foll: Sl 1, k1, psso at beg of needle #1, work in patt to last 2 sts of needle #2, k2tog, sl 1, k1, psso at beg of needle #3, work in patt to last 2 sts of needle #4, k2tog—4 sts dec'd. Working patt as established, dec in this manner every rnd until 6 sts rem. Finish off with a heart of a blossom closure (see page 55).

Thumb: Remove waste yarn and place 16 front sts on needles #1 and #2, and 15 back sts on needles #3 and #4, then pick up 1 st at each end of back sts—33 sts total. Join yarns at right side of opening and foll thumb chart, work across 15 front sts in established hand patt, k2tog with natural, work across 17 back sts, alternating k1 gray, k1 natural in a "salt and pepper" patt—32 sts. Cont in patt until piece measures to middle of thumbnail (about ¾" [2 cm] less than desired total length). **Shape top:** Using the two-wick method as for mitten top, work double-decs until 8 sts rem. Finish off with a heart of a blossom closure. Weave in loose ends. Block.

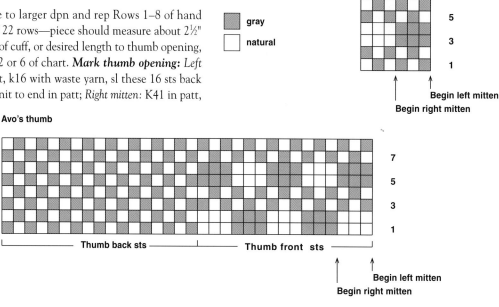

Avo's hand

gray

natural

7
5
3
1

Begin left mitten
Begin right mitten

Avo's thumb

7
5
3
1

Thumb back sts — Thumb front sts

Begin left mitten
Begin right mitten

ELLEN'S STOCKINGS

Ellen Värv is a curator in the Textile Department at the Estonian National Museum in Tartu. She has welcomed me warmly to her museum and also to her home, sharing her knowledge of Estonian textiles and making the entire collection of knitting available to me. Ellen's love for her heritage is inspiring and infectious. I named these stockings for Ellen because she enjoys style and fashion, and is so elegant in a very quiet way.

These stockings are somewhat modern and about as dressy as handknit stockings like these can be. They begin with a double-start cast-on and become a mix of lace stitches and openwork ribbing. The lace runs down the leg and foot, while the ribbing ends part way down the leg. The toe ends in a spiral shape.

Yarn: Satakieli (100% wool; 360 yd [330 m]/100 g): #985 moss green, 1 skein.

Needles: Size 0 (2 mm): Set of 5 double-pointed (dpn).

Gauge: 17 sts and 22 rnds = 2" (5 cm) in St st. Adjust needle size if necessary to obtain the correct gauge.

Finished size: To fit a woman's foot: About 7½" (19 cm) around and 9¾" (25 cm) long.

Leg: Using the double-start method with 2 strands in front and 1 strand in back (see page 42), CO 72 sts. Divide sts evenly onto 4 dpn (18 sts each needle). Using the crossover method (see page 46), join, being careful not to twist sts. Work k1, p1 rib for 3 rnds. Knit 1 rnd, knitting tog the last 2 sts on each needle—68 sts rem (17 sts each needle). Beg with Row 1, work cuff chart over 34 sts (needles #1 and #2) and chevron chart over next 34 sts (needles #3 and #4), noting that the beg of the rnd is at the right side of the cuff chart, not the center back, for a total of 48 rnds, ending with Row 4 of cuff chart and Row 16 of chevron chart—piece should measure about 4¾" (12 cm) from beg. Work 34 back-of-leg sts (needles #1 and #2) in St st and cont chevron patt as established on 34 front sts (needles #3 and #4) until piece measures about 7" (18 cm) from beg or desired length to beg of heel, ending with Row 13 of patt.

Heel: The heel flap is worked on the 34 back-of-leg sts (needles #1 and #2). The rem 34 sts will form the instep. *Heel flap:* Slipping the first st of every row will create chain sts at each edge.

Row 1: (RS) *Sl 1, k33.

Row 2: Sl 1, p33.

Rep Rows 1 and 2 for a total of 34 rows, ending with Row 2 (17 chain sts each edge). ***Turn heel:***

Row 1: (RS) K21, sl 1, k1, psso.

Row 2: Sl 1, p8, p2tog.

Row 3: Sl 1, k8, sl 1, k1, psso.

Rep Rows 2 and 3 until all waiting sts have been used, ending with Row 2—10 heel sts rem.

Foot: (RS) K10 heel sts and with the same needle, pick up and knit 17 sts along left side of heel flap; with 2 other needles, work across 34 held instep sts in chevron patt as established; with rem needle, pick up and knit 17 sts along right

side of heel flap and k5 heel sts—78 sts total; 22 sts each on needles #1 and #4, 17 sts each on needles #2 and #3. Rnd begs at back of heel. *Shape gusset:* Cont in established patt, work as foll:

Rnd 1: Work to last 3 sts on needle #1, k2tog, k1, k34, k1, sl 1, k1, psso, work to end.

Rnd 3: Work even.

Cont to dec 2 sts every other rnd in this manner 5 times total—68 sts rem; 17 sts each needle. Cont as established until foot measures about 8" (20.5 cm) or 2" (5 cm) less than desired total length, ending with Row 5 or 11. Change to St st on all sts and knit 1 rnd. *Shape toe:*

Rnd 1: *Knit to last 2 sts on needle, k2tog; rep from * to end of rnd—4 sts dec'd.

Rnd 2: Knit.

Rep Rnds 1 and 2 a total of 8 times—36 sts rem; 9 sts each needle. Then rep Rnd 1 only until 8 sts rem—2 sts each needle. Finish off with a heart of a blossom closure (see page 55). Weave in loose ends. Block.

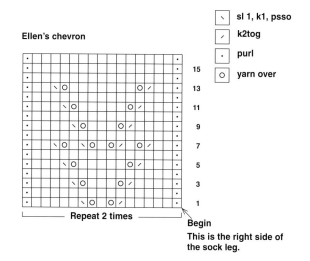

Ellen's chevron

Repeat 2 times

Begin
This is the right side of the sock leg.

sl 1, k1, psso
k2tog
purl
yarn over

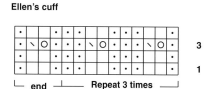

Ellen's cuff

end — Repeat 3 times

HELGI'S MITTENS

These mittens, worked in the card pattern, are named for Helgi Pôllo, the curator at the Hiiumaa Museum in Kassari. Helgi has done extensive research on the knitted mittens of Hiiumaa (one of the larger Estonian islands) and has shared much information with me about their patterns and traditions.

This pair has a classic pattern in classic colors—dark blue and natural. What appears to be small squares with diamonds inside join together to become a series of larger diamonds surrounding eight-point stars. I love this pattern for all the different things it is, depending on how you look at it. The twisted-rib cuff begins with a Continental cast-on and is short, like so many of the old historic mittens of Estonia. The top of the hand and thumb are shaped with two-wick decreases.

73

Yarn: Tuna (100% wool; 350 yd [320 m]/100 g): #3001 natural (MC) and #3013 dark blue, 1 skein each. Small amount of contrasting waste yarn.

Needles: Size 1 (2.25 mm): Set of 5 double-pointed.

Gauge: 16 sts and 19 rnds = 2" (5 cm) in color patt. Adjust needle size if necessary to obtain the correct gauge.

Finished size: To fit a woman's hand; about 9" (23 cm) around and 8½" (21.5 cm) long, excluding cuff.

Cuff: With natural and using the Continental method (see page 41), CO 64 sts. Divide sts evenly onto 4 dpn (16 each needle). Using the crossover method (see page 46), join, being careful not to twist sts. *K1 tbl, p1; rep from *. Work rib in this manner for a total of 7 rnds. Knit 1 rnd, inc 8 sts evenly spaced—72 sts; 18 sts each needle.

Hand: Work Rows 1–18 of hand chart 2 times—piece should measure about 3½" (9 cm) from top of ribbing, or desired length to thumb opening. *Mark thumb opening: Left mitten:* K18 in patt, k15 with waste yarn, sl these 15 sts back onto left needle, knit to end in patt. *Right mitten:* K39 in patt, k15 with waste yarn, sl these 15 sts back onto left needle, knit to end in patt. Cont in patt until piece measures to top of little finger (about 1¾" [4.5 cm] less than desired total length), ending with Row 9 or 18 of chart. *Shape top:* Using the two-wick method (see page 48), work double-decs as foll: *Sl 1, k1, psso at beg of needle #1, work in patt to last 2 sts of needle #2, k2tog, sl 1, k1, psso at beg of needle #3, work in patt to last 2 sts of needle #4, k2tog—4 sts dec'd. Working patt as established, dec in this manner every rnd until 8 sts rem. Finish off with a heart of a blossom closure (see page 55). **Thumb:** Remove waste yarn and place 15 front sts on needles #1 and #2, and 14 back sts on needles #3 and #4—29 sts. Join yarn at right side of opening, pick up and knit 1 st at right front edge, cont according to thumb chart, work 15 front sts in patt, pick up and knit 1 st at left edge, work 14 back sts in patt, pick up and knit 1 st at right back edge—32 sts total; 8 sts each needle. Cont in patt until piece measures to middle of thumbnail (about ¾" [2 cm] less than desired total length), ending with Row 3 or 6 of chart. *Shape top:* Cont in patt and using the two-wick method, work double-decs as for mitten top 3 times—20 sts rem; 5 sts each needle. Cut natural. With blue, work double-decs until 8 sts rem. Finish off with a heart of a blossom closure. Weave in loose ends. Block.

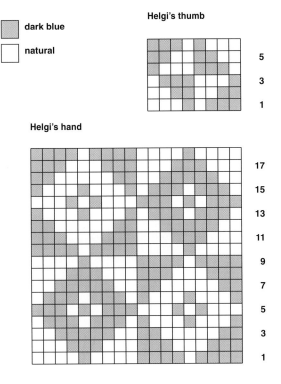

74

Hilja's Mittens

Hilja Aavik is one of the most skilled knitters I've had the fortune to meet in Estonia. She has taught textiles at college and is truly a master. She shared her knowledge with me and opened up a new world of stitches and pattern in the process. I've chosen these mittens as hers because the cuff is lacy and Hilja's true passion is knitted lace.

These mittens were inspired by some from Tõstamaa illustrated in Konsin's book, Slimkoeesemed. The scalloped cuff is seen on many Estonian mittens and gloves. It is known as Vausaba or peacock's tail pattern, and is especially nice when done in color stripes. These mittens begin with a Continental cast-on and finish with a one-wick decrease at the top of the hand and on the thumb.

Yarn: Tuna (100% wool; 350 yd [320 m]/100 g): #3001 natural and #3099 black, 1 skein each; #3024 red and #3002 light gray, partial skein each. Small amount of contrasting waste yarn.

Needles: Size 1 (2.25 mm): Set of 5 double-pointed.

Gauge: 18 sts and 20 rnds = 2" (5 cm) in color patt. Adjust needle size if necessary to obtain the correct gauge.

Finished size: To fit a woman's hand; about 8" (20.5 cm) around and 8" (20.5 cm) long, excluding cuff.

Cuff: With natural and using the Continental method (see page 41), CO 66 sts. Divide sts onto 4 dpn. Using the crossover method (see page 46), join, being careful not to twist sts.

Rnd 1: Knit.

Rnd 2: *K1, yo, k3, k2tog, sl 1, k1, psso, k3, yo; rep from *.

Rep Rnds 1 and 2 for a total of 26 rnds, and *at the same time,* work color stripes as foll: 3 rnds natural, 6 rnds red, 2 rnds light gray, 2 rnds black, 2 rnds light gray, and 11 rnds red. With natural, knit 1 rnd, inc 6 sts evenly spaced—72 sts; 18 sts each needle. With natural, purl 1 rnd.

Hand: Work Rows 1–16 of hand chart, then work Rows 1–7—piece should measure about 2¼" (5.5 cm) from top of cuff, or desired length to thumb opening. ***Mark thumb opening:*** (Row 8 of chart) *Left mitten:* K18 in patt, k16 with waste yarn, sl these 16 sts back onto left needle, knit to end in patt; *Right mitten:* K38 in patt, k16 with waste yarn, sl these 16 sts back onto left needle, knit to end in patt. Work Rows 9–16, then work Rows 1–16 twice—piece should measure to top of little finger (about 1¾" [4.5 cm] less than desired total length). ***Shape top:*** Using the one-wick method (see page 47), work double-dec on last st of needle #4 and first 2 sts on needle #1, and again on the last st on needle #2 and the first 2 sts on needle #3—4 sts dec'd. Working patt as established, dec in this manner every rnd 8 more times, ending with Row 8 of chart—36 sts rem. Cut black. With natural, cont decs until 8 sts rem. Finish off with a heart of a blossom closure (see page 55). ***Thumb:*** Remove waste yarn and place 16 front sts on needles #1 and #2, and 15 back sts on needles #3 and #4—31 sts. Join natural at right side of thumb, pick up and knit 1 st, work across 16 front sts, pick up and knit 1 st at left front thumb edge, join black and work Row 1 of back-of-thumb chart over 15 back sts, with natural, pick up and knit 1 st at right back

thumb edge—34 sts total. Arrange sts so that the 17 front sts (16 live sts plus 1 picked-up st) are on needles #1 and #2, and 17 back sts (15 live sts plus 2 picked-up sts) are on needles #3 and #4. Beg with Row 1, work front sts according to front-of-thumb chart. On next rnd, dec as foll: *Sl 1, k1, psso at beg of needle #1, k2tog at end of needle #2; rep from * across needles #3 and #4—30 sts rem. Work to end of chart—piece should measure to middle of thumbnail (about ¾" [2 cm] less than desired total length). ***Shape top:*** With natural and using the one-wick method as for mitten top, work double-decs until 6 sts rem. Finish off with a heart of a blossom closure. Weave in loose ends. Block.

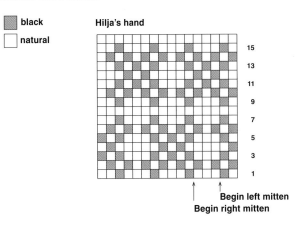

□ black
□ natural

Hilja's hand

15
13
11
9
7
5
3
1

↑ Begin left mitten
Begin right mitten

Hilja's thumb

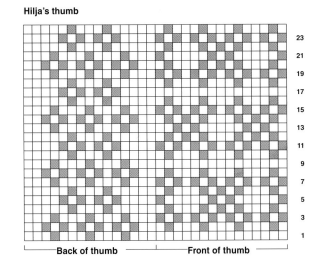

23
21
19
17
15
13
11
9
7
5
3
1

Back of thumb   Front of thumb

Ilmar's Socks

These striped socks are named for Ilmar Kaljurand, a kind man of many talents who seems most happy at his family farm, where he, with his wife Ulla, has created a paradise. As I knitted these socks, I thought of him wearing them to cut wood, to work in the garden, perhaps even to rest in the evening after a good day's work.

My inspiration for these socks was a modern pair I purchased on the island of Hiiumaa. The originals are gray and white and had a "not so intricate" pattern around the calf—I chose to use a more involved pattern and some color changes for this area. The socks begin with a Continental cast-on; the rest is basic knitting, with attention paid to the stripe pattern.

Yarn: Tuna (100% wool; 350 yd [320 m]/100 g): #3020 lamb's brown (MC), #3001 natural (CC), 1 skein each, #3345 madder red, #3109 moss green, partial skein each.

Needles: Size 1 (2.25 mm): Set of 5 double-pointed (dpn).

Gauge: 14 sts and 17 rnds = 2" (5 cm) in striped patt. Adjust needle size if necessary to obtain the correct gauge.

Finished size: To fit a man's foot: About 9½" (24 cm) around and 10¾" (27.5 cm) long.

Leg: With MC and using the Continental method (see page 41), CO 76 sts. Divide sts evenly onto 4 dpn with 18 sts each on needle #1 and #3, and 20 sts each on needle #2 and #4. Using the crossover method (see page 46), join, being careful not to twist sts. Work k2, p2 rib for 10 rnds. Change to CC and work 2 rnds established rib. Change to MC and work 1 rnd as established. Change to CC and work 2 rnds as established. Change to MC and work 2 rnds as established. Beg with Row 1, work leg chart, inc 1 st at the beg and end of needles #1 and #3 on first rnd—80 sts. Work to end of chart. Knit 1 rnd MC. On next rnd, resume k2, p2 rib, dec 1 st at beg and end of needles #1 and #3—76 sts rem. Cont in established rib, working color stripes as foll: 2 rnds MC, 2 rnds CC, 1 rnd MC, 1 rnd CC, 6 rnds MC, [1 rnd CC, 2 rnds MC, 2 rnds CC, 2 rnds MC] 4 times, 1 rnd CC, 2 rnds MC, 2 rnds CC—piece should measure about 9" (23 cm) from beg.

Heel: The heel is worked over 38 back-of-leg sts; the rem 38 sts will form the instep. Note that the seam is along the side of the leg rather than at the back. *Heel flap:* Slipping the first st of every row will create chain sts at each edge.

Row 1: (RS) With MC, *Sl 1, k2; rep from * to last 2 sts, sl 1, k1.

Row 2: Sl 1, p37.

Rep Rows 1 and 2, changing colors at the beg of every RS row for a total of 38 rows, ending with Row 2 (19 chain sts at each edge). *Turn heel:* You will need to break off CC and rejoin it on Row 3 to keep patt continuous.

Row 1: Work 23 sts as established, sl 1, k1, psso.

Row 2: *Sl 1, p8, p2tog.

Row 3: Sl 1, with CC work 8 sts in established patt, sl 1, k1, psso.

Rep Rows 2 and 3, cont to switch colors every RS row,

	madder red
	lamb's brown
	moss green
	natural

Ilmar's leg

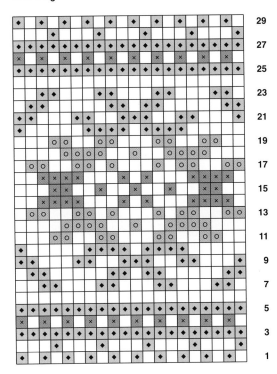

until all the waiting sts have been used, ending with CC and Row 2—10 sts rem.

Foot: The foot is worked in St st in the foll color order: *2 rnds MC, 2 rnds CC, 2 rnds MC, 1 rnd CC; rep from *. With MC, k10 heel sts and with the same needle, pick up and knit 19 sts along left side of heel flap; with 2 other needles work the 38 instep sts (19 sts each needle); with rem needle, pick up and knit 19 sts along right side of heel flap and k5 heel sts—86 sts total; 24 left heel and gusset sts on needle #1, 38 instep sts on needles #2 and #3, 24 right heel and gusset sts on needle #4. Rnd begs at back of heel. **Shape gusset:**

Rnd 1: With MC, work to last 3 sts on needle #1, k2tog, k1, work 38 instep sts, k1, sl 1, k1, psso, work to end.

Rnd 2: Knit, cont in established stripe patt.

Cont to dec 2 sts every other rnd in this manner 7 times total—72 sts rem; 18 sts each needle. Cont as established until foot measures about 3" (7.5 cm) less than desired total length. **Shape toe:** Keeping in established striped patt, dec as foll:

Rnd 1: *K6, k2tog; rep from *—63 sts rem.

Rnds 2–7: Work even.

Rnd 8: *K5, k2tog; rep from *—54 sts rem.

Rnds 9–13: Work even.

Rnd 14: *K4, k2tog; rep from *—45 sts rem.

Rnds 15–18: Work even.

Rnd 19: *K3, k2tog; rep from *—36 sts rem. Cut CC and cont with MC only.

Rnds 20–22: Work even.

Rnd 23: *K2, k2tog; rep from *—27 sts rem.

Rnds 24–25: Work even.

Rnd 26: *K1, k2tog; rep from *—18 sts rem.

Rnd 27: Work even.

Rnd 28: *K2tog; rep from *—9 sts rem.

Finish off with a heart of a blossom closure (see page 55). Weave in loose ends. Block.

JUTA'S STOCKINGS

Yarn: Size small: Koigu Merino (100% wool; 176 yd [161 m]/50 g): #2326 blue, 1 skein. Size medium: Satakieli (100% wool; 357 yd [326 m]/100 g): #132 pale yellow, 1 skein. Size large: Satakieli (100% wool; 357 yd [326 m]/100 g): #251 peach, 1 skein.

Needles: Size 1 (2.25 mm): Set of 5 double-pointed (dpn).

Gauge: 18 sts and 24 rnds = 2" (5 cm) in St st with Koigu Merino; 16 sts and 22 rnds = 2" (5 cm) in St st with Satakieli. Adjust needle size if necessary to obtain the correct gauge.

Finished size: To fit a 1-year old (5-year old, adult) foot: About 5½ (7, 8)" (14 [18, 20.5] cm) around and 5¼ (7¼, 9¾)" (13.5 [18.5, 25] cm) long.

Leg: Using the Continental method (see page 41), CO 48 (56, 64) sts. Divide sts evenly onto 4 dpn with 12 (14, 16) sts each needle. Using the crossover method (see page 46), join, being careful not to twist sts. Work k2, p2 rib until piece measures 1" (2.5 cm) from beg. Knit 1 rnd. Beg lace patt as foll:

Rnd 1: Knit to last 3 sts on needle #1, k2tog, yo, k1, at beg of needle #2, k1, yo, s1, k1, psso, knit to last 3 sts on needle #3, k2tog, yo, k1, at beg of needle #4, k1, yo, s1, k1, psso, knit to end.

Rnds 2, 4, and 6: Knit.

Rnd 3: Knit to last 4 sts on needle #1, k2tog, yo, k2, at beg of needle #2, k2, yo, s1, k1, psso, knit to last 4 sts on needle #3, k2tog, yo, k2, at beg of needle #4, k2, yo, s1, k1, psso, knit to end.

Rnd 5: Knit to last 5 sts on needle #1, k2tog, yo, k3, at beg of needle #2, k3, yo, s1, k1, psso, knit to last 5 sts on needle #3, k2tog, yo, k3, at beg of needle #4, k3, yo, s1 1, k1, psso, knit to end.

Rep Rnds 1–6 until leg measures about 3½ (5½, 7¼)" (9 [14, 18.5] cm) from beg, or desired length to heel, ending with Rnd 6 of patt.

Heel: Rnd begs at center back. **Heel flap:** K12 (14, 16), turn. Sl 1, p23 (27, 31). These 24 (28, 32) sts will form the heel flap; the rem 24 (28, 32) sts will form the instep. Slipping the first st of every row will create chain sts at each edge.

Juta's Stockings

These lacy stockings were inspired by a pair of modern ones I purchased in a shop in Tallinn. They are named after Juta Beauchamp, who is Merike's aunt, Meida's cousin, and Virve's sister-in-law. Juta welcomed me to her home and helped me by translating numerous texts and explaining techniques and difficult words. She also shared the history of her mother, Marta Mäesalu. Marta's story—her life as mother, teacher, scholar, and collector of Estonian traditions—is inspiring and unforgettable.

These stockings begin with a Continental cast-on and are decorated with a lace chevron pattern down the sides of the leg and on top of the foot. I offer them here in three sizes representing, perhaps, the generations of Mäesalu women, their sharing and closeness.

Row 1: (RS) *Sl 1, k1; rep from *.

Row 2: Sl 1, p23 (27, 31).

Rep Rows 1 and 2 for a total of 24 (28, 32) rows, ending with a WS row—12 (14, 16) chain sts each edge. **Turn heel:**

Row 1: (RS) K15 (18, 20), sl 1, k1, psso.

Row 2: Sl 1, p6 (8, 8), p2tog.

Row 3: Sl 1, k6 (8, 8), sl 1, k1, psso.

Rep Rows 2 and 3 until all the waiting sts have been used—8 (10, 10) heel sts rem.

Foot: (RS) K8 (10, 10) heel sts and with the same needle, pick up and knit 12 (14, 16) sts along left side of heel flap; with 2 other needles, work across 24 (28, 32) held instep sts (12 [14, 16] sts on each needle), beg charted patt as foll: Knit to last 3 sts on needle #2, k2tog, yo, k1, at beg of needle #3, k1, yo, sl 1, k1, psso, knit to end of needle #3; with rem needle, pick up and knit 12 (14, 16) sts along right side of heel flap and k4 (5, 5) heel sts—56 (66, 74) sts total; 16 (19, 21) left heel and gusset sts on needle #1, 24 (28, 32) instep sts on needles #2 and #3; 16 (19, 21) right heel and gusset sts on needle #4. Rnd beg at back of heel.

Rnd 1: Work to last 3 sts on needle #1, k2tog, k1, work 24 (28, 32) instep sts in established patt, k1, sl 1, k1, psso, work to end.

Rnd 2: Work even in patt.

Cont to dec 2 sts every other rnd in this manner 4 (5, 5) times—48 (56, 64) sts rem; 12 (14, 16) sts each needle. Cont as established until foot measures about 2" (5 cm) less than desired total length, ending with Rnd 6 of lace patt. Change to St st. **Shape toe:**

Rnd 1: *K6, k2tog; rep from *—42 (49, 56) sts rem.

Rnds 2–5: Knit.

Rnd 6: *K5, k2tog; rep from *—36 (42, 48) sts rem.

Rnds 7–9: Knit.

Rnd 10: *K4, k2tog; rep from *—30 (35, 40) sts rem.

Rnds 11–12: Knit.

Rnd 13: *K3, k2tog; rep from *—24 (28, 32) sts rem.

Rnds 14–15: Knit.

Rnd 16: *K2, k2tog; rep from *—18 (21, 24) sts rem.

Rnd 17: Knit.

Rnd 18: *K1, k2tog; rep from *—12 (14, 16) sts rem.

Rnd 19: Knit.

Rnd 20: *K2tog; rep from *—6 (7, 8) sts rem.

Finish off with a heart of a blossom closure (see page 55). Weave in loose ends. Block.

o yarn over

\ sl 1, k1, psso

/ k2tog

Juta's leg/foot

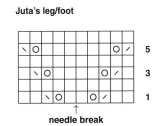

↑
needle break

Kalev's Mittens

These mittens are named for Kalev Ehin, known as Charlie Ehin in his American life. Kalev is a professor of Management at Westminster College in Salt Lake City, and is one of the few Estonians I have the opportunity to meet with on a regular basis. He has helped me translate difficult technical texts and has learned more about knitting than I'm sure he ever wanted.

The pattern used here is the very traditional oaõiekiri or bean blossom pattern from Rapla. The cuff begins with a Continental cast-on and is followed by a k2, p2 corrugated ribbing and a yarnover lateral braid. The top of the mitten ends with a one-wick decrease, as does the thumb, which is worked in a simple broken-stripe pattern.

Yarn: Tuna (100% wool; 350 yd [320 m]/100 g): #3001 natural and #3020 lamb's brown, 1 skein each. Small amount of contrasting waste yarn.

Needles: Size 0 (2 mm): Set of 5 double-pointed.

Gauge: 18 sts and 22 rnds = 2" (5 cm) in color patt. Adjust needle size if necessary to obtain the correct gauge.

Finished size: To fit a man's hand; about 9" (23 cm) around and 9" (23 cm) long, excluding cuff.

Cuff: Leaving a short tail, make a slip knot of both colors and place on needle. Using the Continental method (see page 41) with brown over your thumb and natural over your index finger, CO 80 sts. Divide sts evenly onto 4 dpn (20 sts each needle). Using the crossover method (see page 46), join, being careful not to twist sts. *K2 with brown, p2 with natural; rep from * for a total of 13 rnds—piece should measure 1⅛" (2.8 cm) from beg. With natural and brown, work yarnover braid (see page 49), ending yo with brown, sl 1, k1 with natural, psso—80 sts. Adjust sts so that there are 20 sts on each needle. With brown, knit 1 rnd, inc 1 st at beg of each needle—84 sts; 21 sts on each needle.

Hand: Beg with Row 1, work hand chart for 41 rnds, or desired length to thumb opening. **Mark thumb opening:** *Left mitten:* K23 in patt, k17 with waste yarn, sl these 17 sts back onto left needle and knit them with brown, work to end in patt. *Right mitten:* Keeping in patt, work 44 sts, k17 with waste yarn, sl these 17 sts back onto left needle and knit them with brown, work to end in patt. Cont in patt until piece measures to top of little fingers (about 1¾" [4.5 cm] less than desired total length). **Shape top:** Using the one-wick method (see page 47) and brown for the dec sts, work double-decs on last st of needle #4 and first 2 sts on needle #1, and again on last st on needle #2 and first 2 sts on needle #3—4 sts dec'd. Working patt as established, dec in this manner every rnd until 8 sts rem. Finish off with a heart of a blossom closure (see page 55). **Thumb:** Remove waste yarn and place 17 front sts on needles #1 and #2, and 16 back sts on needles #3 and #4—33 sts. Join brown at left side of opening, pick up and knit 1 st, work back sts according to thumb chart, pick up and knit 1 st at end of back sts, pick up and knit 1 st at beg of front sts, join natural and work to end of front sts according to thumb chart—36 sts total; 9 sts each needle. Join and cont in patt until piece measures to middle of thumbnail (about ¾" [2 cm] less than desired total length). **Shape top:** Cont in patt and using the one-wick method, work double-decs as for mitten top until 8 sts rem. Finish off with a heart of a blossom closure. Weave in loose ends. Block.

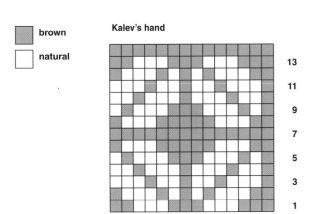

brown
natural

Kalev's hand

13
11
9
7
5
3
1

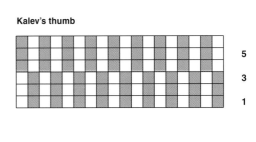

Kalev's thumb

5
3
1

Kristi's Mittens

These colorful mittens were inspired by some I saw pictured in Mulgi Kirikindad ja Kirisukad. They're named for Kristi Paas, a delightful young woman who helped translate the finer points of Estonian knitting during four exciting days at Mardilaat, the St. Martin's Day Festival and Market, in Tallinn.

The hand is decorated with the rattakiri or wheel pattern and the cuff is made in the diagonal "fishtail" pattern that, when colors are changed every three or four rounds, gives the illusion of entrelac. The Continental cast-on is used for this mitten and a "two-wick" decrease in alternating colors shapes the top of the hand and thumb. The colors reflect those described in the Konsin book, Slimkoeesemed.

Yarn: Satakieli (100% wool; 360 yd [329 m]/100 g): #491 old red and #582 purple, 1 skein each. Small amount of contrasting waste yarn.

Needles: Size 0 (2 mm): Set of 5 double-pointed.

Gauge: 18 sts and 22 rnds = 2" (5 cm) in color patt. Adjust needle size if necessary to obtain the correct gauge.

Finished size: To fit a woman's hand; about 8¾" (22 cm) around and 9¼" (23.5 cm) long, excluding cuff.

Cuff: With purple and using the Continental method (see page 41), CO 78 sts. Divide sts evenly onto 4 dpn. Using the crossover method (see page 46), join, being careful not to twist sts. [With purple, *k2, yo, k2, k2tog; rep from * for 4 rnds. With red, rep from * for 4 more rnds] 2 times. With purple, rep first 4 rnds. With purple, knit 1 rnd, inc 2 sts evenly spaced—80 sts total; 20 on each needle.

Hand: Work Rows 1–26 of hand chart, then Rows 1–13—piece should measure about 3½" (9.5 cm) from top of cuff, or desired length to thumb opening. *Mark thumb opening: Left mitten:* K22 in patt, k16 with waste yarn, sl these 16 sts back onto left needle, knit to end in patt. *Right mitten:* K42 in patt, k16 with waste yarn, sl these 16 sts back onto left needle, knit to end in patt. Cont in patt until piece measures to top of little finger (about 1¾" [4.5 cm] less than desired total length). *Shape top:* Using the two-wick method (see page 48), and alternating red and purple for the dec working yarn, work double-decs as foll: Sl 1, k1, psso at beg of needle #1, work in patt to last 2 sts of needle #2, k2tog, sl 1, k1, psso at beg of needle #3, work in patt to last 2 sts of needle #4, k2tog—4 sts dec'd. Working patt as established, dec in this manner every rnd until 8 sts rem. Finish off with a heart of a blossom closure (see page 55). *Thumb:* Remove waste yarn and place 16 front sts on needles #1 and #2, and 15 back sts on needles #3 and #4—31 sts. Join yarns to the right side of the opening and beg with Row 1 of thumb chart, work in patt across the front sts, pick up and knit 1 st at left front edge, work in patt across the back sts, and pick up and knit 2 sts—34 sts total. Work in patt to last 2 sts on needle #2, k2tog, knit to last 2 sts of needle #4, k2tog—32 sts rem; 8 sts each needle. Cont in patt until piece measures to middle of thumbnail (about ¾" [2 cm] less than desired total length). *Shape top:* Cont in patt and using the two-wick method, work double-decs alternating colors as for mitten top until 8 sts rem. Finish off with a heart of a blossom closure. Weave in loose ends. Block.

Kristi's hand

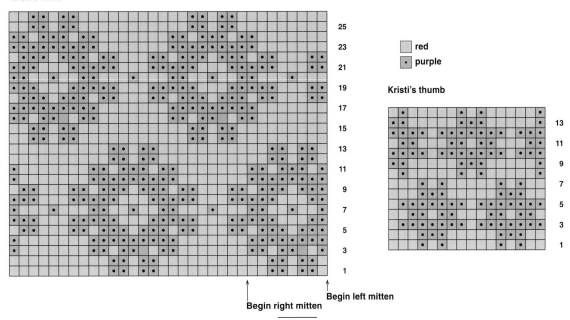

red
• purple

Kristi's thumb

Begin left mitten
Begin right mitten

LAILA'S SOCKS

These socks are named for Laila Pödra, daughter of Aino and Avo. Laila has been chief translator and "emailer extraordinaire" between her mother and myself, helping with subtleties of words and knitting techniques—an interesting feat achieved through cyberspace.

These striped socks were patterned on some in a photograph given to me by Helgi Pôllo, the curator at the Hiiumaa Museum.

There are two different socks in the photo, and I used both of them for inspiration. The larger pattern comes from Emmaste on Hiiumaa and is called Pikad Põrnikad or long beetle or bug. The other similar pattern from Märjamaa is the Vesikilgikiri or water cricket pattern. I didn't worry about where the stripes met at the beginning of the rounds, since I've noticed that many folk knitters weren't the least bothered by little "jogs."

Yarn: Satakieli (100% wool; 357 yd [326 m]/100 g): #199 amber gold (MC) and #003 natural (CC), 1 skein each

Needles: Size 1 (2.25 mm): Set of 5 double-pointed (dpn).

Gauge: 17 sts and 22 rnds = 2" (5 cm) in color patt. Adjust needle size if necessary to obtain the correct gauge.

Finished size: To fit a woman's foot: About 7½" (19 cm) around and 9¼" (23.5 cm) long.

Leg: With MC and using the Continental method (see page 41), CO 72 sts. Divide sts evenly onto 4 dpn (18 sts each needle). Using the crossover method (see page 46), join, being careful not to twist sts. Work k2, p2 rib until piece measures 1¼" (3.2 cm). Knit 1 rnd, dec 2 sts evenly spaced—70 sts total. Arrange sts so there are 18 sts each on needles #1 and #3, and 17 sts each on needles #2 and #4. Beg with Row 1, work leg chart for 63 rnds—piece should measure about 7" (18 cm) from beg.

Heel: Drop CC but do not break off. *Heel flap:* With MC, k18, turn. Sl 1, p34, turn. These 35 sts will form the heel flap; the rem 35 sts will form the instep. Slipping the first st of every row will create chain sts at each edge.

Row 1: (RS) With CC, *sl 1, k1; rep from *, end last rep k2.
Row 2: With CC, sl 1, p34.
Row 3: With MC, *sl 1, k1; rep from *, end last rep k2.
Row 4: With MC, sl 1, p34.

Rep Row 1–4, alternating the colors, for a total of 34 rows, ending with a WS row—17 chain sts each edge. *Turn heel:* With MC only, cont working the heel st (*sl 1, k1; rep from * on RS rows) to give a padded heel and cont the texture on the heel flap as foll:

Row 1: (RS) Work 22 sts in established patt, sl 1, k1, psso.
Row 2: Sl 1, p9, p2tog.
Row 3: Sl 1, [k1, sl 1] 4 times, k1, sl 1, k1, psso.

Rep Rows 2 and 3 until all the waiting sts have been used—11 heel sts rem.

Foot: Note: You'll find it very easy to pick up the gusset sts because the colors alternate down each heel flap edge. Also, as you work the dec rnds, use MC to dec on rnds where both colors are used. With MC, k11 heel sts and with the same needle, pick up and knit 18 sts along left side of heel flap; with 2 other needles, work across the 35 instep sts; with

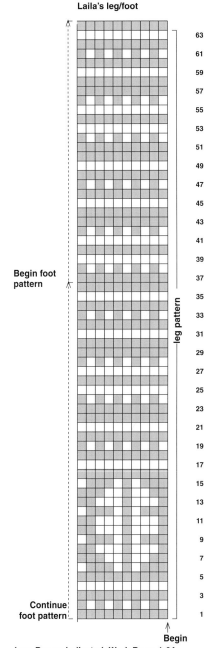

amber gold

natural

Laila's leg/foot

63
61
59
57
55
53
51
49
47
45
43
41
39
37
35
33
31
29
27
25
23
21
19
17
15
13
11
9
7
5
3
1

Begin foot pattern

leg pattern

Begin

Continue foot pattern

Leg: Beg as indicated. Work Rows 1–64. Insert heel.

Foot: Beg at Row 37, work through Row 64, then work Rows 6–36.

rem needle, pick up and knit 18 sts along right side of heel and then k5 heel sts—82 sts total; 24 left heel and gusset sts on needle #1, 17 instep sts on needle #2, 18 instep sts on needle #3, 23 right heel and gusset sts on needle #4. Rnd begs at back of heel. **Shape gusset:** Beg with Row 2 of Foot chart work as foll:

Rnd 1: Work to last 2 sts on needle #1, k2tog (using MC as the working yarn), work across 35 instep sts in patt (beg needle #2 at the beg of the patt, i.e., k1 with CC), s1, k1, psso (using MC as the working yarn), work to end in patt (the st worked after the dec is CC).

Rnd 2: Work even in patt.

Cont to dec 2 sts every other rnd in this manner 6 times total—70 sts rem; 18 sts each on needles #1 and #3, 17 sts each on needles #2 and #4. Cont in patt until foot measures about 2" (5 cm) less than desired total length. Change to MC. **Shape toe:**

Rnd 1: *K5, k2tog; rep from *—60 sts rem.

Rnds 2–6: Knit.

Rnd 7: *K4, k2tog; rep from *—50 sts rem.

Rnds 8–11: Knit.

Rnd 12: *K3, k2tog; rep from *—40 sts rem.

Rnds 13–15: Knit.

Rnd 16: *K2, k2tog; rep from *—30 sts rem.

Rnds 17–18: Knit.

Rnd 19: *K1, k2tog; rep from *—20 sts rem.

Rnd 20: Knit.

Rnd 21: *K2tog; rep from *—10 sts rem.

Finish off with a heart of a blossom closure (see page 55). Weave in loose ends. Block.

LANDRA'S GLOVES

Yarn: Koigu Merino (100% wool;176 yd [160 m]/50g): #0000 natural, 2 skeins; #2238 red, #2343 green, #2191 yellow, and #2174 blue, 1 skein each. Small amount of contrasting waste yarn.

Needles: Size 0 (2 mm): Set of 5 double-pointed.

Gauge: 17 sts and 24 rnds = 2" (5 cm) in St st; 19 sts and 24 rnds = 2" (5 cm) in color patt. Adjust needle size if necessary to obtain the correct gauge.

Finished size: To fit a woman's hand: about 8½" (21.5 cm) around and 9½" (24 cm) long, including cuff.

LEFT GLOVE

Cuff: With natural and using the double-start method with 2 yarns over the thumb (see page 42), CO 70 sts (count the slipknot as 2 sts). Divide sts evenly onto 4 dpn. Using the crossover method (see page 46), join, being careful not to twist sts. Arrange sts so that there are 18 sts each on needles #1 and #3, and 17 sts each on needles #2 and #4. Knit 1 rnd. Beg with Row 1, work cuff chart, inc and dec sts as indicated—72 sts at end of chart. Arrange sts so there are 18 sts on each needle.

Hand: With natural, knit until piece measures ½" (1.3 cm) from top of cuff (about 7 rnds), or desired length to thumb opening. **Mark thumb opening:** K19, k15 with waste yarn, sl these 15 sts back to left needle, work to end. Cont until piece measures 6" (15 cm) from beg, or desired length to base of little finger. **Little finger:** Place last 10 sts on needle #4 onto 1 dpn and first 10 sts on needle #1 onto another dpn for finger. Place rem 52 hand sts onto a length of yarn until needed. K10 palm sts, using the backward loop method (see page 45) CO 4 sts, k10 back-of-hand sts—24 finger sts. Arrange finger sts evenly onto 4 dpn and join into a rnd. Cont until piece measures to middle of fingernail (about ¾" [2 cm] less than desired total length). **Shape top:**

Rnds 1 and 3: With red, knit.

Rnd 2: *K1 blue, k1 green; rep from *.

Rnds 4 and 5: *K1 blue, k3 yellow; rep from *.

Rnd 6: *K1 blue, k2tog yellow, k1 yellow; rep from *—18 sts rem.

Rnd 7: *K1 blue, k2 yellow; rep from *.

Rnd 8: *K1 blue, k2tog yellow; rep from *—12 sts rem.

Rnd 9: *K2tog blue; rep from *—6 sts rem.

Finish off with a heart of a blossom closure (see page 55).

Landra's Gloves

These colorful gloves were inspired by a historic pair from the village of Valjala on the island of Saaremaa. The originals have a pattern on the back of the hand. For my adaptation, I chose to decorate only the cuffs and the tops of the fingers.

These gloves are named not for a person but for a family. Taiu and Maie Landra are a mother/daughter team that designs wonderful knitting patterns and dyes beautiful yarns for their compa-ny, Koigu Wool Designs. These Estonian women, now living in Canada, have carried their heritage forward into their designs, which often include hints of Estonian patterns.

The yarn for these gloves, hand-dyed by Taiu and Maie, is available from Koigu. When knitted, the soft 2-ply Merino wool has a luster and shine. The gloves begin with a double-start cast-on. A three-color twist adds texture to the cuff.

Place 52 held sts onto dpn. Join yarn at left of little finger and work in St st to end, pick up and knit 8 sts along 4 CO sts at base of little finger and join into a rnd—60 sts total. Arrange sts evenly onto 4 dpn and join into a rnd. On next rnd, dec over the 8 picked-up sts at base of little finger as foll: Sl 1, k1, psso, k4, k2tog—58 sts rem. Cont in St st until piece measures ¼" (6 mm) from base of little finger. *Ring finger:* Place the next 8 sts on each side of hand plus the 6 new sts onto dpn—22 sts total. Place rem 36 hand sts onto length of yarn until needed. Beg at left of little finger, k8 palm sts, CO 6 sts, k8 back-of-hand sts, k8—30 sts total. Arrange finger sts evenly onto 4 dpn and join into a rnd. On next rnd, dec over the 8 picked-up sts as foll: Sl 1, k1, psso, k4, k2tog—28 sts rem. Cont in St st until piece measures to middle of fingernail (about ¾" [2 cm] less than total desired length). *Shape top:* Work as for little finger—7 sts rem after Rnd 9. Finish as for little finger. *Middle finger:* Work as for ring finger, casting on 8 sts and picking up 8 sts at base of ring finger, and dec both groups of 8 sts to 6 sts on first rnd. *Index finger:* Place rem 20 sts onto dpn. Join yarn at left of middle finger, k20, pick up and knit 8 sts along 8 CO-sts at base of middle finger—28 sts total. Work as for ring finger. *Thumb:* Remove waste yarn, place 15 front sts onto 2 dpn, 14 back sts onto 2 other dpn, and pick up 1 st at one end of back sts—30 sts. Join natural at right side of opening, k30. Arrange sts evenly onto 4 dpn and join into a rnd. On next rnd, [k14, k2tog] 2 times—28 sts rem. Work as for ring finger. Weave in loose ends. Block.

RIGHT GLOVE

Work cuff and cont in St st to thumb opening as for left glove, working back-of-hand sts on needles #1 and #2, and palm sts on needles #3 and #4. *Mark thumb opening:* K38, k15 with waste yarn, sl these 15 sts back onto left needle, knit to end. Work hand, fingers, and thumb as for left glove.

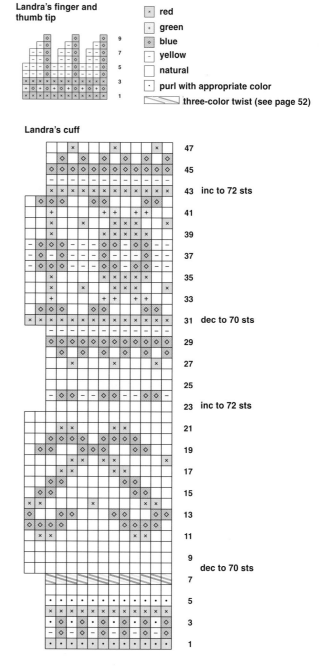

Landra's finger and thumb tip

- □×□ red
- □+□ green
- □◇□ blue
- □−□ yellow
- □ natural
- □·□ purl with appropriate color
- ▨ three-color twist (see page 52)

Landra's cuff

Liidia's Gloves

These gloves are named for Liidia Palu, who lives on Kihnu and who taught me the special braid cast-on used here and which I also named for her. When I met her, Liidia was sitting in front of her farmhouse door, knitting in the warm sun on a summer's afternoon. Our meeting was by chance and is a truly delightful memory for me.

These gloves are fashioned on typical gloves from the island of Kihnu. The cuffs are worked with Kihnu vits braids, a rib pattern, and simple two-colored motif. The hand is worked in a star motif and the fingers and thumb are worked in a smaller, simpler motif.

Yarn: Satakieli (100% wool; 360 yd [329 m]/100 g): #003 natural, #097 black, 1 skein each; #462 red, small amount. Small amount of contrasting waste yarn.

Needles: Size 0 (2 mm): Set of 5 double-pointed.

Gauge: 22 sts and 22 rnds = 2" (5 cm) in color patt.

Finished size: To fit a woman's hand: about 8¼" (21 cm) around by 6½" (16.5 cm) long, excluding cuff.

LEFT GLOVE

Cuff: With white and black and using Liidia's braid method (see page 44), CO 78 sts. Divide sts evenly onto 4 dpn. Using the crossover method (see page 46), join, being careful not to twist sts. Beg with Row 1, work cuff chart, inc 12 sts evenly spaced on Rnd 35—90 sts. Adjust sts so there are 23 sts each on needles #1 and #4, and 22 sts each on needles #2 and #3.

Hand: Work Rows 1–18 of hand chart, then work Row 1 again, or number of rows to desired length to thumb opening. *Mark thumb opening:* K25 in patt, k18 with waste yarn, sl these 18 sts back onto left needle, work to end in established patt. Cont in patt until piece measures 1¾" (4.5 cm) from thumb waste yarn, or desired length to base of little finger. *Little finger:* Place the last 12 sts on needle #4 onto 1 dpn and the first 12 sts on needle #1 onto another dpn for finger. Place rem 66 hand sts onto a length of yarn until needed. With black, k12 palm sts, using the backward loop method

(see page 45) CO 4 sts, k12 back-of-hand sts—28 sts total. Arrange finger sts evenly onto 4 dpn (7 sts each needle) and join into a rnd. Beg with Row 1, work finger and thumb chart for a total of 18 rnds, or until piece measures to middle of fingernail (about ¾" [2 cm] less than desired total length). *Shape top:* Using the two-wick method (see page 48), work double-decs as foll: Sl 1, k1 with black, psso at beg of needle #1, work in patt to last 2 sts of needle #2, k2tog with black, at beg of needle #3, sl 1, k1 with black, psso, work in patt to last 2 sts of needle #4, k2tog with black—4 sts dec'd. Dec in this manner every rnd, alternating black and white for the dec sts until 8 sts rem. Finish off with a heart of a blossom closure (see page 55). *Ring finger:* Place the next 10 sts on each side of the hand onto dpn. Join yarns at left of little finger, work 10 palm sts, CO 6 sts, work 10 back-of-hand sts, pick up and knit 6 sts along 4 CO-sts at base of little finger—32 sts total. Arrange finger sts evenly onto 4 dpn and join into a rnd. Work in established patt until piece measures to middle of fingernail (about ¾" [2 cm] less than desired total length). Finish as for little finger. *Middle finger:* Work as for ring finger, joining yarns at left of ring finger and picking up and knitting sts at base of ring finger—32 sts total. *Index finger:* Place 26 rem sts onto dpn. Work as for ring finger, joining yarns at left of middle finger and picking up and knitting sts at base of middle finger—32 sts total. *Thumb:* Remove waste yarn, place 18 front sts onto 2 dpn, 17 back sts onto 2 other dpn, and pick up 1 st at one end of back sts—36 sts

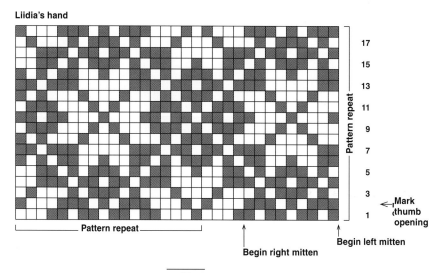

Liidia's hand

17
15
13
11
9
7
5
3
1

Pattern repeat

← Mark thumb opening

⎣—— Pattern repeat ——⎦

Begin right mitten

Begin left mitten

total. Join black at right side of opening. Pick up and knit 1 st, k18, pick up and knit 2 sts, k18, pick up and knit 1 st—40 sts. Arrange sts so there are 10 sts on each dpn. Cont as charted, working tog the first 2 sts on needle #1, the last 2 sts on needle #2, the first 2 sts on needle #3, and the last 2 sts on needle #4—36 sts rem. Work finger and thumb chart until piece measures to middle of thumbnail (about ¾" [2 cm] less than desired total length). **Shape top:** as for fingers. Weave in loose ends. Block.

RIGHT GLOVE

Follow charts, work cuff and cont in hand patt to thumb opening as for left glove, working back-of-hand sts on needles #1 and #2, and palm sts on needles #3 and #4. **Mark thumb opening:** K47 in patt, k18 with waste yarn, sl these 18 sts back onto left needle, knit to end in patt. Work hand, fingers, and thumb as for left glove.

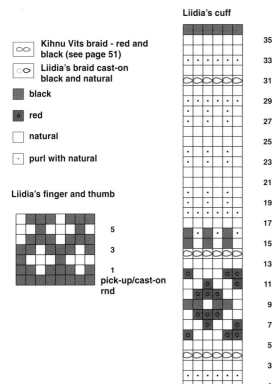

Kihnu Vits braid - red and black (see page 51)

Liidia's braid cast-on black and natural

black

red

natural

purl with natural

Liidia's finger and thumb

LIIVI'S STOCKINGS

Yarn: Tuna (100% wool; 350 yd [320 m]/100 g): #3001 sheep's white (MC), 1 skein; #3020 lamb's brown, half skein; #3345 madder red, #3306 soft yellow, and #3727 light indigo blue, partial skein each.

Needles: Size 0 and 1 (2 mm and 2.25 mm): Set of 5 double-pointed (dpn) each.

Gauge: 16 sts and 18 rows = 2" (5 cm) in color patt on larger needles; 17 sts and 22 rows = 2" (5 cm) in St st on smaller needles. Adjust needle size if necessary to obtain the correct gauge.

Finished size: To fit a woman's foot: about 8" (20.5 cm) around and 9¾" (25 cm) long.

Leg: With brown, smaller needles, and using the Continental method (see page 41), CO 80 sts. Divide sts evenly onto 4 dpn (20 sts each needle). Using the crossover method (see page 46), join, being careful not to twist sts. Work Rows 1–7 of cuff chart. Work St st until piece measures 3¼" (8.5 cm) from beg. Change to larger needles and beg with Row 1, work leg chart, and *at the same time,* when piece measures 5" (12.5 cm) from beg, **Shape leg:** Sl 1, k1, psso, knit to last 2 sts, k2tog—78 sts rem. Dec 2 sts in this manner every 9 rnds 4 times—72 sts rem. Adjust sts so there are 18 sts on each needle. Cont in patt to end of chart. Change to smaller needles, MC, and beg working clocks at each side as foll: *Knit to last 6 sts on needle #1, sl 1, k1, psso, yo, k1, yo, k2tog, k1 at beg of needle #2, k1, sl 1, k1, psso, yo, k1, yo, k2tog, knit to end of needle; rep from * across needles #3 and #4. Cont in this manner until leg measures 13" (33 cm) from beg, or desired length to top of heel.

Heel: *Heel flap:* Work 18 sts, turn. Sl 1, p35. These 36 sts will form the heel; the rem 36 sts will form the instep. Slipping the first st of every row will create chain sts at each edge.
Row 1: (RS) *Sl 1, k1; rep from *.
Row 2: Sl 1, p35.
Rep Rows 1 and 2 for a total of 36 rows, ending with a WS row—18 chain sts at each edge. **Turn heel:**
Row 1: (RS) Work 23 sts as established, sl 1, k1, psso.
Row 2: (WS) Sl 1, p10, p2tog.
Row 3: Sl 1, work 10 sts in patt, sl 1, k1, psso.

Liivi's Stockings

These stockings were inspired by a pair described and illustrated in the first book I discovered about Estonian Folk costume, Eesti Rahvaroivaid. I named them for Liivi Soova, the director of the Estonian Folk Art and Craft Union, and chose them for her because she is involved in many ways with preserving the handcrafts of Estonia. The stockings are from Pärnu-Jaagupi and have many elements found in Estonian knitting in general—colors that could be dyed with plant dyes, stripes of pattern and decoration just so far down the leg, and a solid-colored foot.

They begin with the Continental cast-on, followed by a border of knit and purl stitches. Below the colorwork is a simple openwork clock pattern.

Rep Rows 2 and 3 until all waiting sts have been used—12 sts rem.

Foot: K12 heel sts and with same needle, pick up and knit 18 sts along left side of heel flap; with 2 other needles, work across 36 instep sts as established; with rem needle, pick up and knit 18 sts along right side of heel flap, and k6 heel sts—84 sts total; 24 left heel and gusset sts on needle #1, 18 instep sts each on needles #2 and #3, 24 right heel and gusset sts on needle #4. Rnd begs at back of heel. **Shape gusset:** Cont clock patt as established at beg of needle #2 and end of needle #3.

Rnd 1: Work to last 3 sts on needle #1, k2tog, k1, work 36 instep sts in established patt, sl 1, k1, psso, work to end.

Rnd 2: Work even in patt.

Rep Rnds 1 and 2 a total of 6 times—72 sts rem; 18 sts each needle. Cont even until foot measures about 3¼" (8.5 cm) less than desired total length. Discontinue clock patt. Cont in St st until foot measures about 2¼" (5.5 cm) less than desired total length. **Shape toe:**

Rnd 1: Knit to last 2 sts on needle #1, k2tog, sl 1, k1, psso at beg of needle #2, work to last 2 sts on needle #3, k2tog, at beg of needle #4, sl 1, k1, psso, knit to end.

Rnd 2: Knit.

Rep Rnds 1 and 2 until 36 sts rem—9 sts each needle. Then work Rnd 1 only until 8 sts rem—2 sts each needle. Finish off with a heart of a blossom closure (see page 55). Weave in loose ends. Block.

Liivi's clocks

Liivi's cuff

Liivi's leg

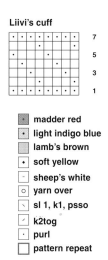

- madder red
- light indigo blue
- lamb's brown
- soft yellow
- sheep's white
- yarn over
- sl 1, k1, psso
- k2tog
- purl
- pattern repeat

beg of dpn #2 and #4 — end of dpn #1 and #3

Beg as indicated. Work in pattern to repeat box, work repeat and decreases as indicated. Work to end of chart in designated colors. Continue with sheep's white only and begin clock patterns.

Maarja's Socks

These fun kid's socks are named after Ellen Värv's daughter, Maarja. Maarja is learning to knit but hasn't become passionate about it yet. She does love to read, and one of her favorite books is Frances Hodgson Burnett's The Secret Garden. I named these stockings for Maarja because they are fun to knit, just as Maarja was fun to meet and share knitting moments with. These socks were inspired by a pair I found in a shop in Tallinn. I love the easy openwork stripes and the bits of added color.

The bold pattern on the leg is one from Hiiumaa, called the Lumeräitsakukiri or snowflake pattern. The cuff begins with a double-start cast-on and the toe ends with a decorative, striped decrease.

Yarn: Satakieli (100% wool; 357 yd [326 m]/100 g): #003 natural and #890 green, half skein each.

Needles: Size 1 (2.25mm): Set of 5 double-pointed (dpn).

Gauge: 18 sts and 22 rnds = 2" (5 cm) in St st. Adjust needle size if necessary to obtain the correct gauge.

Finished size: To fit a child's foot: About 7" (18 cm) around and 7¼" (18.5 cm) long.

Leg: With green and using the double-start method with 2 strands around your thumb and 1 strand around your index finger (see page 42), CO 64 sts. Divide sts evenly onto 4 needles (16 sts each needle). Using the crossover method (see page 46), join, being careful not to twist sts. Work k2, p2 rib for 3 rnds. Beg with Row 1, work leg and foot chart, ending with Row 45—piece should measure about 4" (10 cm) from beg.

Heel: *Heel flap:* Work 16 sts, turn. Sl 1, p31. These 32 sts will form the heel flap; the rem 32 sts will form the instep. Slipping the first st of every row will create chain sts at each edge.

Row 1: (RS) *Sl 1, k1; rep from *.

Row 2: Sl 1, p31.

Rep Rows 1 and 2 for a total of 32 rows, ending with Row 2 (16 chain sts each edge). **Turn heel:** Cont working established heel patt, shape heel as foll:

Row 1: (RS) Work 20 sts as established, sl 1, k1, psso.

Row 2: Sl 1, p8, p2tog.

Row 3: Sl 1, [sl 1, k1] 4 times, sl 1, k1, psso.

Rep Rows 2 and 3 until all waiting sts have been used—10 heel sts rem.

Foot: K10 heel sts and with the same needle, pick up and knit 16 sts along left side of heel flap; with 2 other needles, work across 32 held instep sts (16 sts each needle); with rem needle, pick up and knit 16 sts along right side of heel flap and k5 heel sts—74 sts total; 21 left heel and gusset sts on needle #1, 16 instep sts each on needles #2 and #3, 21 right heel and gusset sts on needle #4. Rnd begs at back of heel.

Shape gusset: Beg with Row 1 of leg and foot chart, work gusset as foll:

Rnd 1: Work to last 2 sts on needle #1, k2tog, k32, sl 1, k1, psso, work to end—72 sts rem.

Cont to dec 2 sts every rnd in this manner 5 times total—64 sts rem; 16 sts each needle. Cont in patt, omitting the tex-

tured patt on Rows 11–14 of the foot chart on needles #1 and #4 (work St st instead) until foot measures about 1" (2.5 cm) less than desired total length, and knitting tog the last 2 sts of the last rnd—63 sts rem.

Shape toe:

Rnd 1: *K7 with natural, k2 with green; rep from *.

Rnd 2: *K6 with natural, k2tog with green, k1 with green; rep from *—56 sts rem.

Rnd 3: *K5 with natural, k2tog with green, k1 with green; rep from *—49 sts rem.

Rnd 4: *K4 with natural, k2tog with green, k1 with green; rep from *—42 sts rem.

Rnds 5–8: Cont in this manner, working 1 less st with natural each rnd—14 sts rem after Rnd 8.

Rnd 9: *K2tog with green; rep from *—7 sts rem.

Finish off with a heart of a blossom closure (see page 55). Weave in loose ends. Block.

Maarja's leg and foot

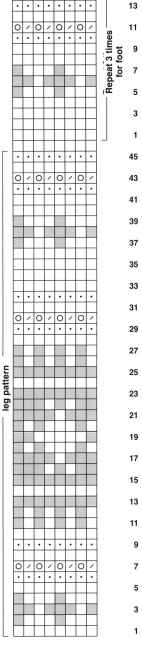

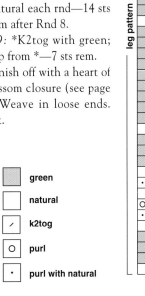

- green
- natural
- k2tog
- purl
- purl with natural

Maimu's Mittens

Maimu Pôldoja is the author of Kudumine, the first Estonian knitting book I studied. I learned many things from this book, among them the nupp (button or bud) stitch, and the fringe cast-on. I have never met Maimu, but have seen much of her knitting, which is truly wonderful. I named these mittens after her because the cuff is decorated with the nupp stitch. The hand is worked in the pôdrasarvekiri or elk horn pattern, which is so very Estonian with its grid outlining the cross motifs. The thumb has a smaller pattern.

The decorative cuff begins with a double-start cast-on and continues with yarnover braids as well as the nupp stitch. The top of the mitten is shaped with half-wick decreases and the thumb is shaped with a rounded finish.

Yarn: Tuna (100% wool; 350 yd [320 m]/100 g): #3020 lamb's brown and #3305 cream, 1 skein each; #3737 yellow-green, partial skein. Small amount of contrasting waste yarn.

Needles: Size 1 (2.25 mm): Set of 5 double-pointed.

Gauge: 16 sts and 18 rnds = 2" (5 cm) in color patt, before blocking. Adjust needle size if necessary to obtain the correct gauge.

Finished size: To fit a woman's hand; about 8" (20.5 cm) around and 6½" (16.5 cm) long, excluding cuff.

Cuff: With brown and using the double-start method with 2 yarns in front and 1 yarn in back (see page 42), CO 64 sts. Divide sts evenly onto 4 dpn (16 sts each needle). Using the crossover method (see page 46), join, being careful not to twist sts. Work Rows 1–30 of chart, working yarnover braids (see page 49), nupp st (see page 54), and dec and inc 1 st as indicated—64 sts after Rnd 30; 16 sts each needle.

Hand: Work Rows 31–46, then Rows 31–32 of chart, or desired length to thumb opening. ***Mark thumb opening:*** *Left mitten:* K18 in patt, k13 with waste yarn, sl these 13 sts back onto left needle, knit to end in patt. *Right mitten:* K34 in patt, k13 with waste yarn, sl these 13 sts back onto left needle, knit to end in patt. Cont working patt rep until piece measures to top of little finger (about 1¾" [4.5 cm] less than desired total length). ***Shape top:*** Using the half-wick method (see page 48) with brown, work double-decs on the last st on needle #4 and first 2 sts on needle 1, and again on the last st on needle #2 and first 2 sts on needle #3—4 sts dec'd. Working patt as established, dec in this manner every rnd until 8 sts rem. Finish off with a heart of a blossom closure (see page 55). ***Thumb:*** Remove waste yarn and place 13 front sts on needles #1 and #2, and 12 back sts on needles #3 and #4—25 sts. Join cream at right side of opening, pick up and knit 1 st at right front edge, work 13 sts according to thumb chart, pick up and knit 2 sts at left side of front sts, work 12 back sts in patt—28 sts total; 7 sts each needle. Join brown and cont thumb chart until piece measures to middle of thumbnail (about ¾" [2 cm] less than desired total length), ending with Row 3 of chart. ***Shape top:*** With brown only, knit 2 rnds. On next rnd, *k2, k2tog; rep from *—21 sts rem. On next rnd, *k1, k2tog; rep from *—14 sts rem. On next rnd, *k2tog; rep from *—7 sts rem. Finish off with a heart of a blossom closure. Weave in loose ends. Block.

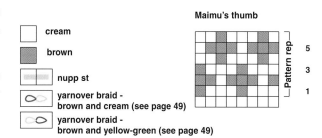

Maimu's thumb

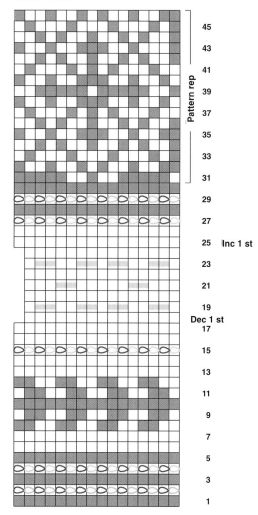

Maimu's hand

Marko's Mittens

These mittens are named for Marko Turban, Estonian athlete and kind and helpful guide and friend to this traveling knitter. Marko didn't get to travel to Kihnu with Anu, Ulla, and me, but he was there in spirit and would have loved it.

These mittens were inspired by the Kihnu style, well illustrated in Ormisson's booklet, Kihnu Kirikindad—with cuffs in many variations of the system seen here and hands decorated in bold geometric patterns. The colors are almost always white and black with red. Take a look behind the thumb for another Estonian treat. This mitten has a Kihnu Troi cast-on, and Kihnu vits lateral braids. The top of the hand and thumb are shaped with one-wick decreases.

Yarn: Tuna (100% wool; 350 yd [320 m]/100 g): #3001 natural and #3099 black, 1 skein each; #3024 red, partial skein. Small amount of contrasting waste yarn.

Needles: Size 0 (2 mm): Set of 5 double-pointed.

Gauge: 18 sts and 21 rnds = 2" (5 cm) in color patt before blocking. Adjust needle size if necessary to obtain the correct gauge.

Finished size: To fit a man's hand; about 9½" (24 cm) around and 8" (20.5 cm) long, excluding cuff.

Cuff: With black and natural and using the Kihnu Troi method (see page 42), CO 64 + 1 sts. Divide sts evenly onto 4 dpn (16 sts each needle). Join as described for this cast-on method, being careful not to twist sts—64 sts rem. Beg with Row 1, work cuff chart, inc 20 sts evenly spaced on Row 33 of chart—84 sts total; 21 sts each needle.

Hand: Work Rows 1–22 of hand chart—piece should measure about 2" (5 cm) from top of cuff, or desired length to thumb opening. *Mark thumb opening:* (Rnd 1 of chart) *Left mitten:* K24 in patt, k16 with waste yarn, sl these 16 sts back onto left needle, knit to end in patt; *Right mitten:* K44

in patt, k16 with waste yarn, sl these 16 sts back onto left needle, knit to end in patt. Cont in patt until piece measures to top of little finger (about 2½" [6.5 cm] less than desired total length). *Shape top:* Using the one-wick method (see page 47), work double-dec with black on last st of needle #4 and first 2 sts on needle #1, and again on last st on needle #2 and first 2 sts on needle #3—4 sts dec'd. Dec in this manner every rnd, working patt as established, until 8 sts rem. Finish off with a heart of a blossom closure (see page 55). *Thumb:* Remove waste yarn and place 16 front sts on needles #1 and #2, and 15 back sts on needles #3 and #4—31 sts. Join yarns to right side of thumb opening, pick up and knit 1 st at beg of front sts, work 16 front sts as charted, pick up and knit 2 sts at beg of back sts, beg with Row 1, work 15 back sts as charted, pick up and knit 1 st at end of back sts—35 sts total; 18 back sts and 17 front sts. Cont in patt until piece measures to middle of thumbnail (about ¾" [2 cm] less than desired total length). *Shape top:* Cont in patt as charted and using the one-wick method, work double-decs with black as for mitten top until 8 sts rem. Finish off with a heart of a blossom closure. Weave in loose ends. Block.

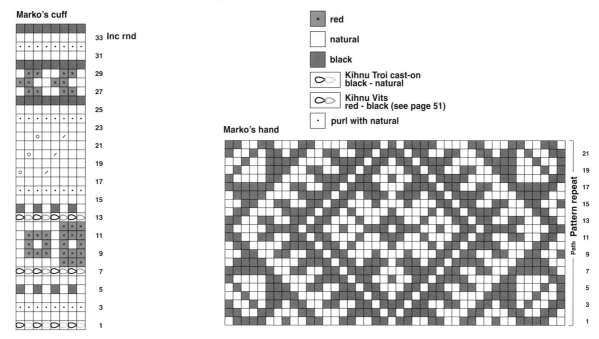

Marko's cuff

Marko's hand

red

natural

black

Kihnu Troi cast-on
black - natural

Kihnu Vits
red - black (see page 51)

purl with natural

Marko's left thumb

Marko's right thumb

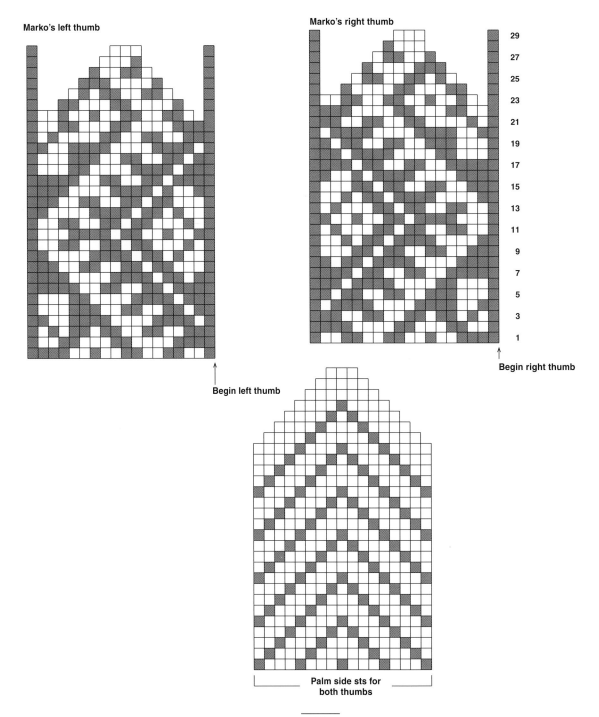

29
27
25
23
21
19
17
15
13
11
9
7
5
3
1

Begin right thumb

Begin left thumb

Palm side sts for both thumbs

Meida's Mittens

This mitten design was inspired by one from the village of Helme. The original is pictured in Konsin's book, Slimkoeesemed *and also in* Mulgi Kirikindad ja Kirisukad. *It is named for Meida Jöeveer, a dear friend who has offered advice, support, lodging, and delicious meals during my visits to* her wondrous land. I think she would like the colors in the cuff very much.

This mitten has a Continental cast-on, begins with three rounds of k2, p2 rib in green and blue, and finishes with a two-wick decrease at the top and thumb.

Meida's cuff

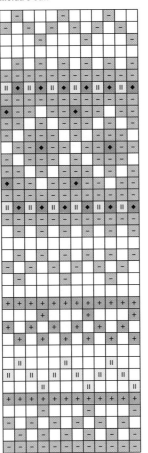

- natural
- || moss green
- − dark blue
- + madder red
- ◆ red-purple

Yarn: Tuna (100% wool; 350 yd [320 m]/100 g): #3001 natural, 1 skein; #3013 dark blue, #3321 reddish purple, #3345 madder red, and #3109 moss green, partial skein each. Small amount of contrasting waste yarn.

Needles: Size 1 (2.25 mm): Set of 5 double-pointed.

Gauge: 16 sts and 21 rnds = 2" (5 cm) in St st before blocking. Adjust needle size if necessary to obtain the correct gauge.

Finished size: To fit a woman's hand; about 9" (23 cm) around and 6½" (16.5 cm) long, excluding cuff.

Cuff: With green and using the Continental method (see page 41), CO 72 sts. Divide sts evenly onto 4 dpn (18 sts on each needle). Using the crossover method (see page 46), join, being careful not to twist sts. With green, knit 1 rnd. Work 3 rnds corrugated ribbing as foll: *k2 with dark blue, p2 with green; rep from *. Beg with Row 1, work to end of cuff chart.

Hand: With natural, work St st for 18 rnds, or desired length to thumb opening. *Mark thumb opening: Left mitten:* K20, k15 with waste yarn, sl these 15 sts back onto left needle, knit to end; *Right mitten:* K37, k15 with waste yarn, sl these 15 sts back onto left needle, knit to end. Cont in St st until piece measures to top of little finger (about 1½" [3.8 cm] less than desired total length). *Shape top:* Using the two-wick method (see page 48), work double-decs as foll: Sl 1, k1, psso at beg of needle #1, knit to last 2 sts of needle #2, k2tog, sl 1, k1, psso at beg of needle #3, knit to last 2 sts of needle #4, k2tog—4 sts dec'd. Dec in this manner every rnd until 8 sts rem. Finish off with a heart of a blossom closure (see page 55). *Thumb:* Remove waste yarn and place 15 front sts on needles #1 and #2, and 14 back sts on needles #3 and #4—29 sts. Join yarn to right side of opening, pick up and knit 1 st at right front edge, k15 front sts, pick up and knit 2 sts at left side of front sts, k14 back sts—32 sts total; 8 sts on each needle. On the next rnd, k2tog, k14, k2tog, k14—30 sts rem. Cont in St st until thumb measures to middle of thumbnail (about ¾" [2 cm] less than desired total length). *Shape top:* Using the two-wick method as for mitten top, work double-decs until 6 sts rem. Finish off with a heart of a blossom closure. Weave in loose ends. Block.

Merike's Gloves

These elegant gloves are named for Merike Nichols, the friend who took me to Estonia for the first time, introduced me to her native country, and opened so many doors for me. We were at the market in Kuressaare on the island of Saaremaa when I first saw this type of glove, and we shared our delight in it. The traveling-stitch patterning (made by moving one stitch over another) is known as *vikkel* in Estonian.

These gloves begin with a double-start cast-on. The thumbs have decorative gusset shapings, which are more common on gloves than mittens in Estonia, worked with yarnovers.

Yarn: Koigu Merino (100% wool; 176 yd [160 m]/50 g): #0000 natural, 2 skeins. Small amount of contrasting waste yarn.

Needles: Size 0 (2 mm): Set of 5 double-pointed.

Gauge: 16 sts and 24 rnds = 2 (5 cm) in St st. Adjust needle size if necessary to obtain the correct gauge.

Finished size: To fit a woman's hand: about 8" (20.5 cm) around and 7½" (19 cm) long, excluding cuff.

LEFT GLOVE

Cuff: Using the double-start method with 2 yarns over the thumb (see page 42), CO 72 sts (count the slipknot as the first st). Divide sts evenly onto 4 dpn. Using the crossover method (see page 46), join, being careful not to twist sts. Arrange sts so there are 18 sts on each needle (palm sts on needles #1 and #2; back-of-hand sts on needles #3 and #4). Knit 1 rnd. Purl 1 rnd. *Set up rnd:* [K1, p1, k6, p1, k2, p1, k4, p1, k2, p1, k4, p1, k2, p2, k6, p1, k1] 2 times. Work cuff chart until piece measures 2¼" (5.5 cm) from beg or desired cuff length.

Hand: *K26 (palm sts), cont in established patt across back-of-hand sts. Rep from * for a total of 3 rnds. **Thumb gusset:** Note: Sl markers on all rnds.

Rnd 1: K26, yo, place marker (pm), work 10 sts as established, pm, yo, work to end as established.

Rnds 2–6 and 8–12: Knit to m, work 10 sts as established, work to end as established.

Rnds 7 and 13: Knit to m, yo, work 10 sts as established, yo, work to end as established—78 sts after Rnd 13.

Cont as established until piece measures 2¼" (5.5 cm) from top of cuff or desired length to thumb opening. **Mark thumb opening:** K26, k16 with waste yarn, sl these 16 sts back onto left needle, k16, work to end in established patt. [Work 1 rnd in patt. On next rnd, k27, sl 1, k1, psso, k10, k2tog, work to end in patt] 2 times—74 sts rem. Cont as established until piece measures 4" (10 cm) from top of cuff or desired length to base of little finger. **Little finger:** Place last 10 sts on needle #4 onto 1 dpn and first 10 sts on needle #1 onto another dpn for finger. Place rem 54 hand sts on a length of yarn until needed. K10 palm sts, using the backward loop method (see page 45) CO 5 sts, k10 back-of-hand sts—25 sts total. Arrange finger sts evenly onto 4 dpn and

join into a rnd. Cont in established patt until piece measures 4 rnds (about ½" [1.3 cm]) less than desired total length. *Shape top:*

Rnds 1 and 3: Work even in patt.

Rnd 2: *K1, k2tog; rep from *, end k1—17 sts rem.

Rnd 4: *K2tog; rep from *, end k1—9 sts rem.

Finish with a heart of a blossom closure (see page 55). Place 54 held sts onto dpn. Join yarn at left of little finger and work sts as established, pick up and knit 7 sts along 5 CO sts—61 sts total. On next rnd, dec in the 7 picked-up sts as foll: Sl 1, k1, psso, k3, k2tog—59 sts rem. Cont in patt for 3 more rnds. **Ring finger:** Place the next 8 sts on each side of the hand plus the 5 new sts onto dpn. Place rem 38 hand sts onto a length of yarn until needed. Beg at left of little finger, k8 palm sts, CO 6 sts, k8 back-of-hand sts, k5—27 sts total. Arrange sts evenly onto 4 dpn and join into a rnd. Cont in patt until piece measures to middle of fingernail (about ¾" [2 cm] less than desired total length). **Shape top:**

Rnds 1, 3, and 5: Work even in patt.

Rnd 2: *K2, k2tog; rep from *, end k1, k2tog—20 sts rem.

Rnd 4: *K1, k2tog; rep from *, end k2—14 sts rem.

Rnd 6: *K2tog; rep from *—7 sts rem.

Finish with a heart of a blossom closure. **Middle finger:** Place next 8 sts from each side of the hand plus the 6 new sts onto dpn. Place rem 22 sts onto a length of yarn until needled. Join yarn at left of ring finger. K8 palm sts, CO 6 sts, work 8 back-of-hand sts, pick up and knit 7 sts into the 6 CO-sts at base of ring finger—29 sts total. Join into a rnd. On next rnd, dec the 7 picked-up sts as foll: Sl 1, k1, psso, k3, k2tog—27 sts rem. Work as for ring finger. **Index finger:** Place 22 rem sts onto dpn. Join yarn to left of middle finger, work 22 sts in patt, pick up and knit 7 sts in the 6 CO-sts at base of middle finger—29 sts total. Work as for ring finger. **Thumb:** Remove waste yarn, place 16 front sts onto 2 dpn, 15 back sts onto 2 other dpn, and pick up 1 st at one end of back sts—32 sts. Join yarn at right side of opening, pick up and knit 1 st, work 16 front sts in patt, pick up and knit 2 sts, work 16 back sts, pick up and knit 1 st—36 sts total. Arrange sts so there are 9 sts on each needle. Sl 1, k1, psso at beg of needle #1, knit to last 2 sts of needle #2, k2tog, sl 1, k1, psso at beg of needle #3, knit to last 2 sts of needle #4, k2tog—32 sts rem. Cont in established patt until piece measures to middle of thumbnail (about ¾" [2 cm] less than desired total length). *Shape top:*

Rnds 1, 3, and 5: Knit.

Rnd 2: *K2, k2tog; rep from *—24 sts rem.

Rnd 4: *K1, k2tog; rep from *—16 sts rem.

Rnd 6: *K2tog; rep from *—8 sts rem.

Finish off with a heart of a blossom closure. Weave in loose ends. Block.

RIGHT GLOVE

Work cuff as for left glove, working back-of-hand sts on needles #1 and #2, and palm sts on needles #3 and #4. Set up hand as foll: Work 46 sts in patt, k26 (palm sts). Work as for left glove to thumb gusset. *Thumb gusset:*

Rnd 1: Work 36 sts in established patt, yo, pm, work 10 sts in established patt, pm, yo, knit to end.

Rnds 2–6 and 8–12: Work in patt to m, work 10 sts as established, knit to end.

Rnds 7 and 13: Work in patt to m, yo, work 10 sts as established, yo, knit to end—78 sts after Rnd 13.

Cont as for left glove to thumb opening. *Mark thumb opening:* K36, with waste yarn k16, sl these 16 sts back onto left needle, knit to end. [Work 1 rnd even in patt. On next rnd, k37, sl 1, k1, psso, k10, k2tog, k1, knit to end] 2 times. Work hand, fingers, and thumb as for left glove.

⧄⧄ k2tog, knit first st again

⧄⧄ knit tbl of second st, knit first st

▢ pattern repeat

⋅ purl

Merike's cuff

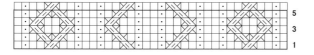

5
3
1

Rita's Stockings

Yarn: Satakieli (100% wool; 357 yd [326 m]/100 g): #003 natural, 1 skein; #966 blue and #462 red, partial skein each.

Needles: Size 0 (2 mm): Set of 5 double-pointed (dpn).

Gauge: 17 sts and 22 rnds = 2" (5 cm) in color patt; 16 sts and 14 rnds = 2" (5 cm) in St st. Adjust needle size if necessary to obtain the correct gauge.

Finished size: To fit a woman's foot: About 7½" (19 cm) around and 9¼" (23.5 cm) long.

Leg: With natural and using the Kihnu Troi method (see page 42), CO 80 + 1 sts. Divide sts evenly onto 4 dpn (20 sts each needle). Join as described for this cast-on method, being careful not to twist sts—80 sts rem. Knit 1 rnd, purl 1 rnd. Work Kihnu vits as foll:

Rnd 1: *K1 with blue, k1 with red; rep from *.

Rnd 2: Bring both colors to the front as to purl, *p1 (the blue st) with red, p1 (the red st) with blue; rep from *, bringing each color *under* the other every time you change colors.

Knit 1 rnd with natural. Beg with Row 1, work cuff chart, dec 4 sts evenly spaced on Row 14—76 sts. Arrange sts so there are 19 sts on each needle and the rnd beg at the back of the leg. Beg with Row 1, work leg chart, dec 4 sts evenly spaced on Row 27 (knit the last 2 sts tog at the end of each needle)—72 sts rem; 18 sts each needle. Cont through Row 30 of chart. Change to natural only. *Set up clock patts:* Beg with Rnd 1 of patts, work as foll: K11, work left-cross clock chart over next 16 sts, k18, work right-cross clock chart over next 16 sts, k11. Cont patts as established until leg measures about 8" (20.5 cm) from beg, or desired length to top of heel, ending with Row 7 of diagonal clock patts.

Heel: *Heel flap:* Keeping knit-purl clocks as established, work heel flap as foll: Work 18 sts on needle #1 in patt, turn. Sl 1, work 35 sts in established patt. These 36 sts, (from needles #1 and #4) will form the heel flap; the rem 36 sts will form the instep. Slipping the first st of every row will create chain sts at each edge.

Row 1: (RS) Sl 1, work 35 sts as established.

Row 2: Sl 1, work 35 sts as established.

Rep Rows 1 and 2 for a total of 36 rows, ending with Row 2 (18 chain sts each edge). *Turn heel:*

RITA'S STOCKINGS

*T*hese technique-filled stockings are named to honor my friend and helpful translator, Rita Tubalkain. Rita is an embroider-er and knitter of great skill. She has taken the patterns of her native Estonia and embroidered them onto cloth and knitted them into warm hand coverings, putting her love for her land in every stitch. Rita translated Konsin's book Slimkoeedemed for me, solving mysteries that otherwise would have been forever hidden.

These stockings begin with a Kihnu Troi cast-on, followed by a Kihnu vits braid. Next comes a simple lace section, which causes the top to scallop. The color work section is typically Estonian—the Xs and Os are akin to Shetland patterning. The leg is decorated with clocks—one side is knit and purl, the other has vikkel, or traveling, stitches.

Row 1: (RS) Work 23 sts as established, sl 1, k1, psso.

Row 2: Sl 1, p10, p2tog.

Row 3: Sl 1, k10, sl 1, k1, psso.

Rep Rows 2 and 3 until all waiting sts have been used, ending with Row 2—12 heel sts rem.

Foot: K12 heel sts and with same needle, pick up and knit 18 sts along left side of heel flap; with 2 other needles, work across 36 held instep sts as established; with rem needle, pick up and knit 18 sts along right side of heel flap and k6 heel sts—84 sts total; 24 left heel and gusset sts on needle #1, 18 instep sts each on needles #2 and #3, 24 right heel and gusset sts on needle #4. Rnd beg at back of heel. **Shape gusset:** Cont clock patt as established at beg of needle #2 and end of needle #3.

Rnd 1: Work to last 3 on needle #1, k2tog, k1, work 36 instep sts, k1, sl 1, k1, psso, work to end.

Rnd 2: Work even in patt.

Cont to dec 2 sts every other rnd in this manner 6 times total—72 sts rem; 18 sts each needle. Cont in patt until foot measures about 1½" (3.8 cm) less than desired total length. Knit 1 rnd. **Shape toe:**

Rnd 1: *K4, k2tog; rep from *—60 sts rem.

Rnds 2–5: Knit.

Rnd 6: *K3, k2tog; rep from *—48 sts rem.

Rnds 7–10: Knit.

Rnd 11: *K2, k2tog; rep from *—36 sts rem.

Rnds 12–13: Knit.

Rnd 14: *K1, k2tog; rep from *—24 sts rem.

Rnd 15: Knit.

Rnd 16: *K2tog; rep from *—12 sts rem.

Rnd 17: Knit.

Rnd 18: *K2tog; rep from *—6 sts rem.

Finish off with a heart of a blossom closure (see page 55). Weave in loose ends. Block.

☐	natural
■	red
⊠	blue
·	purl
○	yarn over
⋋	sl 1, k2tog, psso
☐	pattern repeat

⧄⧄ k2tog, knit first st again

⧅⧅ knit tbl of second st, knit first st

Rita's leg

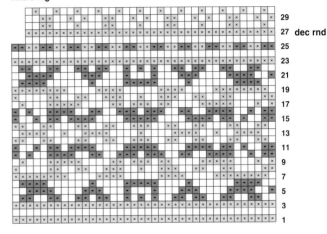

Rita's left-cross clock

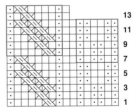

Rita's right-cross clock

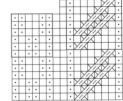

Rita's cuff

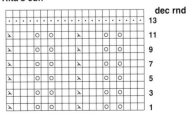

Sander's Mittens

Sander is the son of Ellen Värv, the curator at the Estonian National Museum in Tartu. While he is surely wearing adult-sized mittens by now, these mittens would have suited him when he was younger.

A Continental cast-on begins the mitten and the cuff is worked in the "fishtail" pattern. The hand is worked in the Kassikäpakiri or cat's paw pattern and finishes with a one-wick decrease. The thumb is worked in a simpler, diamond-shaped design and finishes with a two-wick decrease. I chose these two endings because each works best with the pattern below it.

Yarn: Satakieli (100% wool; 360 yd [329 m]/100 g): #003 natural, #890 green, and #966 blue, ½ skein each. Small amount of contrasting waste yarn.

Needles: Size 0 (2 mm): Set of 5 double-pointed.

Gauge: 18 sts and 22 rnds = 2" (5 cm) in color pattern. Adjust needle size if necessary to obtain the correct gauge.

Finished size: To fit a child's hand; about 6¼" (16 cm) around and 5½" (14 cm) long, excluding cuff.

Cuff: With blue and using the Continental method (see page 41), CO 54 sts. Divide sts evenly onto 4 dpn. Using the crossover method (see page 46), join, being careful not to twist sts. *K2, yo, k2, k2tog; rep from * for 3 rnds. With natural, work 4 rnds as established. With green, work 4 rnds as established. With natural, work 4 rnds as established. With blue, work 4 rnds as established. With natural, knit 1 rnd, inc 2 sts evenly spaced—56 sts; 14 sts each needle.

Hand: Work Rows 1–16 of hand chart, then Rows 1–3—piece should measure about 3½" (9.5 cm) from top of cuff, or desired length to thumb opening, ending with Row 3. *Mark thumb opening:* (Row 4 of chart) *Left mitten:* K16 in patt, k11 with waste yarn, sl these 11 sts back onto left needle, knit to end in patt. *Right mitten:* K29 in patt, k11 with waste yarn, sl these 11 sts back onto left needle, knit to end in patt. Cont in patt until piece measures to top of little finger (about 1" [2.5 cm] less than desired total length), ending with Row 15 of chart. *Shape top:* (Row 16 of chart) With natural and using the one-wick method (see page 47), work as foll: work double-dec on last st on needle #4 and first 2 sts on needle #1, and again on last st on needle #2 and first 2 sts on needle #3—4 sts dec'd. Working patt as established, dec in this manner every rnd until you've completed Row 7 of chart. With natural only, cont working decs until 8 sts rem. Finish off with a heart of a blossom closure (see page 55). *Thumb:* Remove waste yarn and place 11 front sts on needles #1 and #2, and 10 back sts on needles #3 and #4. Join natural and k11 front sts, pick up and knit 2 sts, work 10 back sts according to thumb chart, pick up and knit 1 st with natural—24 sts total; 6 sts each needle. Cont in patt until piece measures to middle of thumbnail—piece should measure about 1¼" (3.2 cm) from beg (about ½" [1.3 cm] less than desired total length). *Shape top:* Using the two-wick method

(see page 48) and natural, work double-decs as foll: Sl 1, k1, psso at beg of needle #1, knit to last 2 sts of needle #2, k2tog, sl 1, k1, psso at beg of needle #3, knit to last 2 sts of needle #4, k2tog—4 sts dec'd. Dec in this manner every rnd, working patt as established, until 8 sts rem. Finish off with a heart of a blossom closure. Weave in loose ends. Block.

green

blue

natural

Sander's hand

Sander's thumb

Tiit's Socks

These socks are named for Meida's son, Tiit Jöeveer. This kind man was part of the group that met me when I first stepped onto Estonian soil, off a boat from Helsinki, and has been a welcoming host and fabulous cook for later visits. I have memories of a very special birthday party, thanks to Tiit!

These socks are decorated with the Kitsisilmakiri or goat's eye pattern. They begin with a Continental cast-on and have k2, p2 ribbing before the leg pattern begins. The heel flap is worked with slipped stitches offset every other right-side row. The toe decrease has a left-leaning decrease (s1 1, k1, psso), a plain knit stitch, and a right-leaning decrease (k2tog) at each side of the toe. Though a bit unconventional, the finished product is neat and tidy.

Yarn: Tuna (100% wool; 350 yd [320 m]/100 g): #3002 light gray (MC) and #3012 indigo blue, 1 skein each.

Needles: Size 1 (2.25 mm): Set of 5 double-pointed (dpn).

Gauge: 16 sts and 18 rnds = 2" (5 cm) in color patt. Adjust needle size if necessary to obtain the correct gauge.

Finished size: To fit a man's foot: About 8½" (21.5 cm) around and 10½" (26.5 cm) long.

Leg: With gray and using the Continental method (see page 41), CO 72 sts. Divide sts evenly onto 4 needles (18 sts each needle). Using the crossover method (see page 46), join, being careful not to twist sts. Rnd beg at back of leg. Work k2, p2 rib until piece measures 3" (7.5 cm). Join blue and knit 1 rnd, then work 2 rnds in established rib. With gray, knit 1 rnd, then work 4 rnds in established rib. With blue, knit 1 rnd, then work 2 rnds in established rib. With gray, knit 1 rnd, then work 7 rnds in established rib. Beg with Row 1, work leg and foot chart until piece measures 8½" (21.5 cm) or desired length to beg of heel, ending with Row 5 of patt. Adjust sts so there are 18 sts each on needles #1 and #2, 19 sts on needle #3, and 17 sts on needle #4.

Heel: *Heel flap:* With gray, k18 sts, turn. Sl 1, p34. These 35 sts will form the heel flap; the rem 37 sts will form the instep. Slipping the first st of every row will create chain sts at each edge.

Row 1: *Sl 1, k1; rep from *, end last rep k2.

Rows 2 and 4: Sl 1, p34.

Row 3: Sl 1, *Sl 1, k1; rep from *.

Rep Rows 1–4 for a total of 38 rows, ending with a WS row (19 chain sts each edge). *Turn heel:*

Row 1: (RS) Work 21 sts as established, sl 1, k1, psso.

Row 2: Sl 1, p7, p2tog.

Row 3: Sl 1, k7, sl 1, k1, psso.

Rep Rows 2 and 3 until all waiting sts have been used—9 sts rem.

Foot: On the next rnd, you will pick up and knit sts using both colors to cont established patt down the foot. Begin by working across the 4 heel sts (rnd will beg at center of heel). Join blue and cont in established patt (using both colors) as foll: K2 blue, k2 gray, pick up and knit 19 sts along left side of heel flap as foll: 3 gray, 3 blue, 5 gray, 3 blue, 5 gray, work

instep sts as established (note that the patt will be interrupted bet needles #1 and #2, and again bet needles #3 and #4), pick up and knit 17 sts (skipping 2 chain sts evenly spaced to get correct st count) along right side of heel flap as foll: 5 gray, 3 blue, 5 gray, 3 blue, 1 gray, work rem 5 heel sts as foll: k4 gray, k1 blue—82 sts total; 23 left heel and gusset sts on needle #1, 18 instep sts on needle #2, 19 instep sts on needle #3, 22 right heel and gusset sts on needle #4. Rnd beg at back of heel. *Shape gusset:* Note: Always work the decs with gray.

Rnd 1: Work in patt to last 2 sts on needle #1, k2tog, work 37 instep sts in patt, sl 1, k1, psso, work to end in patt.

Rnd 2: Work even in patt.

Cont to dec 2 sts every other rnd in this manner 5 times total—72 sts rem; 18 sts each on needles #1 and #2, 19 sts on needle #3, and 17 sts on needle #4. Cont even in patt until foot measures about 7½" (19 cm) or 2" (5 cm) less than desired total length, ending with Row 1 of patt. Arrange sts so there are 18 sts on each needle (rnd begs at the center of the bottom of the foot). *Shape toe:* Note: Use gray for working all decs and the single knit st bet decs.

Rnd 1: Keeping in patt, work to last 3 sts on needle #1, sl 1, k1, psso, k1, at beg of needle #2, k2tog, work in patt to last 3 sts on needle #3, sl 1, k1, psso, k1, at beg of needle #4, k2tog, work to end.

Rep Rnd 1 a total of 14 times—16 sts rem; 4 sts each needle. Change to gray only, and cont decs as established until 8 sts rem; 2 sts each needle. Finish off with a heart of a blossom closure (see page 55). Weave in loose ends. Block.

■ indigo blue

□ light gray

Tiit's leg and foot

9

7

←end leg pat; beg heel

5

3

1

Ulla's Gloves

These gloves are named for Ulla Kaljurand, who has been a wonderful guide, travel companion, and friend, and with whom I spent a delightful afternoon in Tõstamaa, lunching in a small cafe. Roositud translates as "rose" pattern, and I used it here because when I think of Ulla, I think of the beautiful bouquets of wild flowers that she gathered from the woods near her farm.

The decorative patterning is similar to patterns I saw in the Estonian National Museum in Tartu and in Konsin's book, Slimkoeesemed, from Tõstamaa. The originals have a fringe where the cuff meets the hand. I chose to work a fringe at the beginning only and used the roositud inlay on the cuff and hand, and textured patterns on the little finger and thumb to echo patterns on the originals.

Yarn: Finullgarn (100% wool; 180 yd [164 m]/50 g): #404 light gray (MC), 2 skeins. Strikkegarn (100% wool; 96 yd [88 m]/50 g): #150 gold, #146 pumpkin, and #181 rust, small amounts of each. Small amount of contrasting waste yarn.

Needles: Size 00 (1.75 mm): Set of 5 double-pointed.

Gauge: 17 sts and 26 rnds = 2" (5 cm) in St st. Adjust needle size if necessary to obtain the correct gauge.

Finished size: To fit a woman's hand: about 8½" (21.5 cm) around and 6¾" (17 cm) long, excluding cuff.

LEFT GLOVE

Cuff: With gray and using the fringe method (see page 44), CO 72 sts. (Beg with a slipknot and make 36 looped fringes to equal 73 sts total.) Divide sts evenly onto 4 dpn. Using the extra stitch method (see page 46), join, being careful not to twist sts. Arrange sts so that there are 18 sts on each needle (palm sts on needles #1 and #2; back-of-hand sts on needles #3 and #4). Work Rows 1–27 of cuff chart, working roositud inlay (see page 52) and vikkel braid (see page 50; remembering to replace a st on the left needle after working each set of twisted sts, and ending the braid by slipping the first st onto the right needle, binding the last st off over it, and then replacing the st onto the left needle) as indicated.

Hand: Knit 6 rnds. Work 36 sts on needles #1 and #2. Beg with Row 1 and foll directions on back-of-hand chart, work roositud inlay as indicated (inlay begs on 13th st of needle #3) and little finger patt rep (worked on last 7 sts of needle #4). Work as charted until piece measures 1½" (3.8 cm) from top of cuff (about 17 rnds total), or desired length to thumb opening. **Mark thumb opening:** K20, k14 with waste yarn, sl these 14 sts back onto left needle, work to end in established patt. Cont until piece measures 1¾" (4.5 cm) from thumb waste yarn, or desired length to base of little finger. **Little finger:** Place last 8 sts on needle #4 onto 1 dpn and first 8 sts on needle #1 onto another dpn for finger. Place rem 56 hand sts onto a length of yarn until needle. K8 palm sts, using the backward loop method (see page 45) CO 4 sts, k8 back-of-hand sts—20 sts total. Arrange finger sts evenly onto 4 dpn and join into a rnd. Work in established patt until piece measures to middle of fingernail (about ¾" [2 cm] less

than desired total length). **Shape top:**

Rnd 1: *K1, k2tog; rep from *, end k2—14 sts rem.

Rnd 2: Knit.

Rnd 3: *K2tog; rep from *—7 sts rem.

Finish off with a heart of a blossom closure (see page 55). Place 56 held hand sts onto dpn. Join yarn at left of little finger and work in St st to end. Pick up and knit 6 sts along 4 CO-sts at base of little finger, and join into a rnd—62 sts. Arrange finger sts evenly onto 4 dpn and join into a rnd. On next rnd, dec over the 6 picked-up sts as foll: Sl 1, k1, psso, k2, k2tog—60 sts. Work in St st until piece measures ¼" (6 mm) from base of little finger. **Ring finger:** Place the next 8 sts on each side of the hand plus the 4 new sts onto dpn. Place rem 40 hand sts on a length of yarn until needed. Beg at left of little finger, k8 palm sts, CO 4 sts, k8 back-of-hand sts, k4—24 sts total. Arrange finger sts evenly onto 4 dpn and join into a rnd. Work in St st until piece measures to middle of fingernail (about ¾" [2 cm] less than desired total length). *Shape top:*

Rnd 1: *K1, k2tog; rep from *, end k2—16 sts rem.

Rnd 2: Knit.

Rnd 3: *K2tog; rep from *—8 sts rem.

Finish off with a heart of a blossom closure. **Middle finger:** Place the next 9 sts on each side of the hand plus the 4 new sts onto dpn. Place rem 22 sts onto a length of yarn until needed. Join yarn at left of ring finger. K9 palm sts, CO 4 sts, work across back-of-hand sts, pick up and knit 6 sts along 4 CO-sts at base of ring finger, and join into a rnd—28 sts total. On next rnd, dec over the 6 picked-up sts as foll: Sl 1, k1, psso, k2, k2tog—26 sts rem. Work in St st until piece measures to middle of fingernail (about ¾" [2 cm] less than total desired length). *Shape top:*

Rnd 1: *K2, k2tog; rep from *, end k2—20 sts rem.

Rnd 2: Knit.

Rnd 3: *K1, k2tog; rep from *, end k2—14 sts rem.

Rnd 4: *K2tog; rep from *—7 sts rem.

Finish off with a heart of a blossom closure. **Index finger:** Place rem 22 sts onto dpn. Join yarn at left of middle finger, k22, pick up and knit 6 sts along 4 CO-sts at base of middle finger—28 sts total. On next rnd, dec the 6 picked-up sts to 4 as before—26 sts rem. Work to end as for middle finger. **Thumb:** Remove waste yarn, place 14 front sts onto 2 dpn, 13 back sts onto 2 other dpn, and pick up 1 st at one end of back sts—28 sts. Join yarn at right side of opening, pick up and knit 1 st, k14, pick up and knit 2 sts, k14, pick up and knit 1 st—32 sts total. Arrange sts evenly onto 4 dpn and join into a rnd. *Next rnd:* Sl 1, k1, psso, knit to last 2 sts on needle #2, k2tog, sl 1, k1, psso at beg of needle #3, work to last 2 sts on needle #4, k2tog—28 sts total. Work little finger centered over thumb sts until piece measures to middle of thumbnail (about ¾" [2 cm] less than desired total length).

Shape top:

Rnd 1: *K2, k2tog; rep from *—21 sts rem.

Rnd 2: Knit.

Rnd 3: *K1, k2tog; rep from *—14 sts rem.

Rnd 4: *K2tog; rep from *—7 sts rem.

Finish off with a heart of a blossom closure. Weave in loose ends, making 1 or 2 fringe loops with the CO tail to fill in the gap at the bottom edge. Block.

RIGHT GLOVE

Following charts, work cuff and cont in hand patt to thumb opening as for left glove, working back-of-hand sts on needles #1 and #2, and palm sts on needles #3 and #4. Set up little finger and roositud patts as indicated on chart. **Mark thumb opening:** Work 38 sts in patt, k14 with waste yarn, sl these 14 sts back onto left needle, knit to end. Work hand, fingers, and thumb as for left glove.

gray	
root	
pumpkin	
gold	
purl with gray	
vikkel braid (see page 50)	

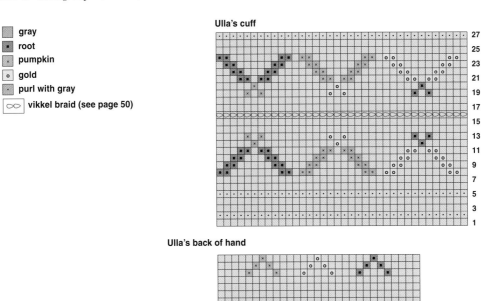

Ulla's cuff

Ulla's back of hand

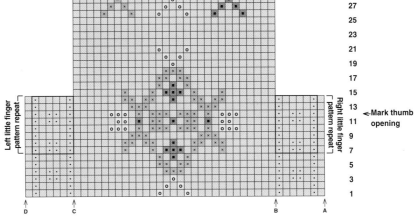

Left glove: Work palm sts. Begin at B (needle #3), end at D working little finger pattern repeat for entire length. Right glove: Begin at A (needle #1), work little finger pattern repeat for entire length, end at C, work palm sts.

Left little finger pattern repeat

Right little finger pattern repeat

←Mark thumb opening

VIRVE'S STOCKINGS

This design is from the village of Halliste. I found it in the book, Slimkoeesemed, by K. Konsin, and later saw a pair of the same design at the Estonian National Museum. I named these stockings for Virve Mäesalu, who gave me a copy of Konsin's book, a gift that has meant so much to me. Virve is Merike's aunt, Juta's sister-in-law, and Meida's cousin—a wonderful Estonian family that has shared with me the delights of their culture.

These stockings begin with a double-start cast-on, followed by an openwork border. The leg is plain, except for a band of patterning near the ankle. Some of the oldest knitting found in Estonia, now in the Estonian National Museum in Tartu, has a similar pattern.

Yarn: Tuna (100% wool; 350 yd [320 m]/100 g): #3001 natural (MC), 1 skein; #3737 yellow-green, #3730 dark gray, and #3010 leaf green, partial skein each.

Needles: Size 0 and 1 (2 mm and 2.25 mm): Set of 5 double-pointed (dpn) each.

Gauge: 16 sts and 22 rnds = 2" (5 cm) in St st. Adjust needle size if necessary to obtain the correct gauge.

Finished size: To fit a woman's foot: About 8½" (21.5 cm) around and 9½" (24 cm) long.

Leg: With smaller needles, MC, and using the double-start method with a single strand over your finger and thumb (see page 42), CO 91 sts. Divide sts evenly onto 4 needles. Using the crossover method (see page 46), join, being careful not to twist sts. Purl 1 rnd. Beg with Row 1, work through Row 18 of cuff chart. Note: You must move the first st of rnd back to the last needle on every odd-numbered rnd to maintain correct st count on each needle. Change to St st and dec 3 sts evenly spaced—88 sts rem. Arrange sts so there are 22 sts each needle. Cont even until piece measures 4" (10 cm) from beg. *Shape leg:*

Rnd 1: Sl 1, k1, psso, knit to last 2 sts, k2tog—2 sts dec'd.
Rnds 2–8: Knit.

Rep Rnds 1–8 a total 8 times—72 sts rem. Knit 8 rnds. Change to larger needles and beg with Row 1, work through Row 17 of leg chart. Change to smaller needles and cont in St st with natural until piece measures about 15" (38 cm) or desired length to top of heel.

Heel: *Heel flap:* K18, turn. Sl 1, p35. These 36 sts will form the heel (the rem 36 instep sts will be used later). Slipping the first st of every row will create chain sts at each edge.
Row 1: (RS) Sl 1, k35.
Row 2: (WS) Sl 1, p35.

Rep Rows 1 and 2 for a total of 32 rows—16 chain sts at each edge. *Turn heel:*
Row 1: (RS) K23, sl 1, k1, psso.
Row 2: Sl 1, p10, p2tog.
Row 3: Sl 1, k10, sl 1, k1, psso.

Rep Rows 2 and 3 until all waiting sts have been used, ending with Row 2—12 heel sts rem.

Foot: K12 and with the same needle, pick up and knit 16 sts along left side of heel; with 2 other needles k36 instep sts; with rem needle, pick up and knit 18 sts along right side of heel flap and k6 heel sts—82 sts total; 22 left heel and gusset sts on needle #1, 18 instep sts each on needles #2 and #3, 22 right heel and gusset sts on needle #4. Rnd begs at back of heel. *Shape gusset:*

Rnd 1: Knit to last 3 sts on needle #1, k2tog, k1, k36 instep sts, sl 1, k1, psso, knit to end.
Rnd 2: Knit.

Rep Rnds 1 and 2 a total 4 times—72 sts rem; 18 sts each needle. Cont even in St st until foot measures about 2¼" (5.5 cm) less than desired total length. *Shape toe:*

Rnd 1: Knit to last 2 sts on needle #1, sl 1, k1, psso; k2tog at beg of needle #2; knit to last 2 sts on needle #3, sl 1, k1, psso; k2tog at beg of needle #4, work to end.
Rnd 2: Knit.

Rep Rnds 1 and 2 a total of 9 times—36 sts rem; 9 sts each needle. Then rep Rnd 1 only until 8 sts rem—2 sts each needle. Finish off with a heart of a blossom closure (see page 55). Weave in loose ends. Block.

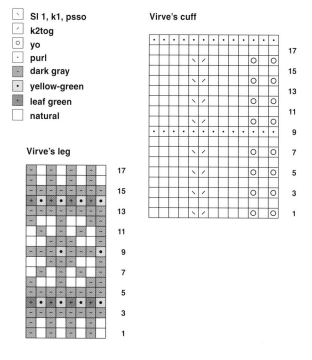

- SI 1, k1, psso
- k2tog
- yo
- purl
- dark gray
- yellow-green
- leaf green
- natural

Virve's cuff

Virve's leg

Bibliography

Aasma, Karin. "Folklig stickning i Estland" (Folk Knitting in Estonia), *Hemslöjden* Nr 2. Stockholm: Svenska Hemslöjdsföreningarnas Riksförbund, 1984.

Belitser, V., T. Habicht etal., editors. *Eesti Rahvaroivaid. XIX Sajandist ja XX Sajandi algult.* Tallinn: Eesti Riiklik Kirjastus, 1957.

Etnograafia Muuseum. *Mulgi Kirikindad ja Kirisukad.* Tallinn: Eesti Kiiklik Kirjastus, 1960.

Gottfridsson, Inger and Ingrid Gottfridsson. *The Swedish Mitten Book: Traditional Patterns from Gotland.* Ashville, North Carolina: Lark Books, 1984.

Gustafsson, Kerstin. *Gamla Textila Tekniker i Ull (Old Textile Techniques in Wool).* Helsingborg, Sweden: LTS Publishing Co., 1988.

Hallik, Claire. *Silmus Kudumine.* Tallinn: Eesti Riiklik Kirjastus, 1957.

Hein, Anne, Liivia Kivilo, etal. *Käsitöö.* Tallinn: Valgus, 1995.

Kaarma, Melanie and Aino Voolmaa. *Eesti Rahvaroivaid.* Tallinn: Eesti Raamat, 1981.

Kivilo, Liivia. "Sokid", and "Kindad", 1992. (Leaflets)

Konsin, Kalju. *Eesti Rahvakunst.* Tallinn: Valgus, 1970.

——. *Koekirjalised Kindad Ja Sukad.* Tartu: Eesti NSV Riiklik Etnograafiamuuseum, 1969.

——. *Slimkoeesemed.* Tallinn: Kirjastus Kunst, 1972.

Land, People and Culture. Permanent Exhibition of Everyday Life at the Estonian National Museum, notes from the ERM Web Site, 1996.

Manninen, I. *Eesti Rahvariiete Ajalugu.* Tartu: Eesti Rahva Muuseumi, 1927.

——. *Kindad.* Tartu: Etnograafilised Monograafiad, 1927.

Martinson, Kate. "Scandinavian Nålbinding." *The Weaver's Journal.* Vol. XII, Number 2, Issue 46. St. Paul, Minnesota: Arana Press Inc., Fall 1987.

Meeri, Tiina. *Kudumisõpetus (vol 2).* Tallinn: Valgus, 1997.

Nordland, Odd. *Primitive Scandinavian Textiles in Knotless Netting.* Oslo: Oslo University Press, 1961.

Nylen, Anna-Maja. Translated by Anne-Charlotte Hanes Harvey. *Swedish Handcraft.* Lund, Sweden: Håkan Ohlssons Förlag, 1976.

Ormisson, Heli. *Kihnu Kirikindad.* Pärnu: Varten, 1994.

Paulson, Ivar. *The Old Estonian Folk Religion.* Uralic and Altaic Series, vol. 108. Bloomington, Indiana: Indiana University Publications, 1971.

Peets, Juri. *Totenhandschuhe im Bestattungsbrauchtum der Esten und anderer. Ostseefinnen from Fennoscandia Archaelogica IV.* Helsinki, 1987.

——. *Eesti arheoloogilised tekstiilid kalmetest ja peitleidudest III-XVI saj. Magistritöö.* (M.A. thesis), Tartu, 1992.

——. "Mõista, mõista, mis see on–üks maja, viis kambrit?" (Guess, guess, what is it—one house, five chambers?) *Horisont*, pps. 18 – 20, 1991.

Põldoja, Maimu. *Kudumine.* Tallinn: Valgus, 1992.

Pöhl-Andersen, Ingeborg. *Flitiga Händer.* Stockholm: Norstedts Tryckeri AB, 1994.

Põllo, Helgi. *Hiiumaa Kindakirjad 1.* Kärdla: AS DAGOsent.

Puhvel, Madli. *Symbol of Dawn.* Tartu: Tartu University Press, 1995.

Ränk, Gustav. *Old Estonia, People and Culture.* Bloomington, Indiana: Indiana University Press, 1976.

Raun, Linda. "Subcontractor's Monograph on the Estonians." Prepared by faculty and staff of Indiana University's Graduate program in Uralic and Asian Studies. New Haven, Connecticut: Human Relations Area Files, Inc., 1955.

Raun, Toivo U. *Estonia and The Estonians.* Stanford, California: Hoover Institution Press, Stanford University, 1987.

Reimann, Leili. *Pitsilised Koekirjad.* Tallinn: Valgus, 1978 abd 1986.

Runge, Ene. "Estonia." Lecture given at the Royal Ontario Museum in October, 1984.

Sihvrele, Mare and Valve Alamaale. *Mulgi Kindad.* Pärnu: Väljaandja Oü Heili Kirjastus, 1998.

Stengård, Hermanna. *Gotländsk Sticksöm.* Stockholm: Albert Bonniers Förlag, 1925.

Tedre, Ulo. *Estonian Customs and Traditions*, English translation. Tallinn: Perioodika Publishers, 1991.

Turnau, Irena, translated by Agnieszka Szonert. *History of Knitting Before Mass Production.* Warszawa: Oficyna Wydawnicza, AKCENT, 1991.

Tuubel, Vivre. "Hiiumaa Kindad", *Nõukogude Naine* #11, 1988.

Värv, Ellen. *Estonian Folk Costume.* Tallinn: Estonian Institute, 1998.

Viires, Ants. *Eesti Rahvakultuuri Leksikon.* Tallinn: Eesti Entsüklopeediakirjastus, 1995.

Yarn Sources

A special thank you to Lars at Unicorn, Meg at Schoolhouse Press, Deb at Nordic Fiber Arts and Taiu and Maie at Koigu for making all the great yarns used in this book available.

Satakieli
Schoolhouse Press, 6899 Cary Bluff. Pittsville, WI 54466, (715) 884-2799 (retail only)

Koigu Merino
Koigu Designs, R.R. #1, Williamsford, Ontario, Canada, NOH 2VO, (519) 794-306 (wholesale and retail)

Tuna
Unicorn Books and Crafts, 1338 Ross Street, Petaluma, California 94954, (707) 762-3362 (wholesale only)

Rauma Finullgarn and Strikkegarn
Nordic Fiber Arts, Four Cutts Road, Durham, New Hampshire 03824, (603) 868-1196 (wholesale and retail)

All yarns are also available through
The Wooly West, 1417 South 1100 East, Salt Lake City, Utah 84105, (801) 487-9378 (retail only)

Index

abbreviations 58
Aino's Gloves 59–61
All Soul's Day 15
Anu's Christmas Gloves 62–64
Anu's Mittens 64–66
Anu's Stockings 66–68
Avo's Mittens 69–70
backward loop cast-on 45
birth and childhood 18
braids 49–52
calendar sticks 12
Candlemas 11, 16
cast-ons 41–45
continental cast-on 41–42
crossover join 46
decreases 47–48
double-start cast-on 42
dyes 33–34
Easter 14
Ellen's Stockings 71–72
end of life 24
Epiphany 16
extra stitch join 46
fringe cast-on 44–45
half-wick decrease 48
heart of a blossom closure 55
Helgi's Mittens 73–74
Hilja's Mittens 75–86
Ilmar's Socks 77–79
Juta's Stockings 79–81
Kalev's Mittens 82–83
Kihnu troi cast-on 42–43
Kihnu vits braid 51–52

knitting as sacrifice, magic, and medicine 24–25
Koidula, Lydia 9
Konsin 28, 39
Kristi's Mittens 84–85
Lady Day 14
Laila's Socks 86–88
Landra's Gloves 88–90
leggings 37–38
Liidia's braid cast-on 44
Liidia's Gloves 91–93
Liivi's Stockings 93–95
Maarja's Socks 96–97
Maimu's Mittens 98–99
Manninen 39
Marko's Mittens 100–102
marriage customs 18–24
Meida's Mittens 103–104
Merike's Gloves 105–107
Michaelmas 11, 12, 15
Midwinter 17
mittens and gloves, historic 33–37
nålbinding 26–27
National Awakening 9–10
New Year 16
nupp stitch 54–55
one-wick decrease 47–48
Peets, 26–27, 33
Ränk 11, 21
Raun, L. 8, 9
Raun, T. 8, 11
Rita's Stockings 107–109
roositud 36, 39, 40, 52–53

runic calendar 12
Sander's Mittens 110–111
Shrove Tuesday 17
socks and stockings, historic 37–40
Sowing Day 11
St George's Day 12
St. Andrew's Day 15
St. Anthony's Day 11, 16
St. Catherine's Day 15
St. George's Day 14
St. Jacob's Day 14
St. John's Day 11, 12, 14
St. Martin's Day 15
St. Michael's Day 11, 12, 15
St. Nicholas's Day 11
St. Olaf's Day 14
St. Thomas' Day 16
Tedre 11, 19, 20, 21, 23
thumb openings 54
Tiit's Socks 112–113
traveling stitch braid 50–51
Twelfth Day 16
two-end join 46
two-wick decrease 48–49
Ulla's Gloves 114–116
vikkel braid 50–51
vikkel pattern 36, 49, 53–54
Vivre's Stockings 117–119
wick decreases 47–49
Winter Crest Day 11
yarnover braid 49–50
Yellowing Day 11